INNER PEACE NOW

OTHER MATERIALS BY DR. KIRK LAMAN

Books:
How to Heal Your Broken Heart
Stressed Out Heart
Overcome Your Daily Stress
Your Blueprint for Anxiety Relief

Video Training.
Quick Anxiety Relief
Quick Stress Relief
Tranquil Heart

Audio Training.
Stress Relief for Your Heart
Stress and Heart Disease- The Hidden Link
Healing Your Heart

The Video and Audio trainings can be found at:
https://drkirklaman.com/courses-2/

A SIMPLE GUIDE TO FEELING CALM AND HAPPY

INNER PEACE NOW

Dr. KIRK LAMAN
Whole Hearted Cardiologist

Copyright © Kirk Laman 2024

All Rights Reserved. No part of this book may be reproduced by any means without the prior written permission of the author, except for short passages used in reviews.

Digital Version Inner Peace Now: ISBN: 978-0-9883941-2-4
Hardcover: Inner Peace Now: ISBN. 978-0-9883941-3-1
Soft Cover: Inner Peace Now: ISBN. ISBN: 978-0-9883941-4-8

Praise be to the All-Loving, All-Merciful Creator
The One, The Irresistible.
Nothing Moves Without His Loving Touch

To My Guide –Muhammad bin-Yahya Ninowy
A light of love and peace in the world.
To my Guide – Muhammad ar-Rifa'i
May his Secret be Perfumed.

And to My Lovely Wife Hassna
Whose Love and Support Makes Everything Possible

ACKNOWLEDGMENTS

Thank you to Laurie Chittenden, Reedsy editor, for her expert reading and editing of the first draft of the manuscript. Thanks to Sierra Burroughs, my fellow MFA classmate, for her evaluation and insights into the book. A heartfelt thank you to Amina al-Jamal, editor and publisher of *Sidi Muhammad Press*, for her recommendations and input on the manuscript. A special thanks to Shaykh Muhammad bin Yahya Al-Ninowy for his reading and recommendation of portions of the manuscript. The biggest thanks to Gabriel Aziz (name changed) for allowing his healing journey to be recorded and published. You are a strong and brave soul. My hat is off to you. Your openness and willingness to let your story help others is remarkable.

DISCLAIMER

This manuscript is written for educational and informational purposes only. It is not intended, nor should it be used, to diagnose or treat any medical or psychological condition or as a substitute for professional medical advice, treatment, or care. The information provided does not establish a doctor-patient relationship. Please consult your healthcare provider before utilizing this book's emotional/spiritual techniques. The user of techniques and methods offered in this book is solely responsible for the outcomes. We don't make any guarantees about the results of using these techniques.

The persons depicted in this non-fiction work are real. The healing sessions displayed in this book occurred as written. A minor degree of literary license was utilized to facilitate the flow of the story. The names of the persons involved have been changed to protect their identity.

TABLE OF CONTENTS

1. Dancing in the Storm 9
2. The Path of Love. 25
3. Open the Door of Awareness 55
4. Reflect Upon Your Life. 77
5. Return to Your Heart. 95
6. Embrace Self-Forgiveness. 115
7. Extend Forgiveness to Others 129
8. Practice Gratitude 143
9. Give Yourself Hope and Mercy. 157
10. *The Remembrance* the Key to Healing 171
11. Develop a Daily Heart Connection Practice 199
12. Ride the Waves 211
13. Where to Go from Here. 223
Afterword 227
Appendix: How to Practice *The Remembrance* 229
Endnotes 235

INTRODUCTION

The crying erupted from deep within my heart. Spasms of primordial weeping, like the moans of a strange jungle animal, burst from my lungs. I was sitting on the floor of my living room. Twenty or thirty people, primarily strangers, packed the room. They stared at me, eyes darting from me back to the holy man perched at the front of the room. No one said anything. The holy man glanced furtively at me. The corners of his mouth rounded in a half-smile. He nodded as if he knew what was happening but did not attempt to stifle my cries.

I thought, *Why Me? Why now?*

The words cascaded inside.

A forty-year-old man bursting into spasms of tears should have provoked feelings of humiliation. Still, as a cardiologist who had taken care of thousands of patients, many of them suffering from severe life-shattering illnesses, I understood that intense emotions often erupted in public places. I had experienced it in packed hospital hallways and waiting rooms; I had consoled countless wives, husbands, parents, and children who had suffered the loss of someone they held dear.

Raw emotion had driven out my shame. The last ten years of my marriage had been a disaster. I felt trapped in a relationship that couldn't be changed or saved. My children were young. They needed my presence and support, and I didn't dare to leave. I endured the daily feeling of watching my life pass me by. My inner torment had led me to the holy man and had propelled me on an inner spiritual journey. Now I was in a crowd of mostly strangers crying uncontrollably.

My heart was churning in a way I had never experienced. Wave after wave of inexplicable, rushing emotional movements—sadness, frustration, and inner perplexity, boiled inside, bursting forth in a torrent of tears.

Perhaps you feel this way or have felt this way.

Maybe you are one of the many millions of people living with trepidation. Perhaps your life has been battered by a storm—a ferocious storm caused by adverse life experiences: anxiety, depression, sadness, terror, hopelessness, panic attacks, or worry. You wonder, "Why Me? When will this end?"

Countless people feel similarly distressed. Their hearts yearn for relief. They crave a safe harbor from the hurricane-force winds of life. So they search. They scan the internet. Social media obsesses them—Facebook, Instagram, TikTok, and Twitter. They yearn for a book, a course, or a program to calm the anxiety that racks their psyche. Their hearts long to be rid of the difficulties ravishing their lives. They are looking for a voice to guide them and a way to connect with others.

On that fall afternoon twenty-eight years ago, I was moved in a way I couldn't understand or explain. It was like my heart was a giant egg, filled with unresolved aching, torment, and grief. And it was being cracked, rap, rap, rap, on the edge of a red-hot skillet. And with each strike, emotional sorrow would seep out. Droplets of sadness would fall to the sizzling surface, become scorched, and instantly vaporize into tears. And so I

Introduction

cried, weeping for over four hours. At times, the tears would slacken, but then the inner churning would build. My heart wound tighter and tighter, seeking something inside that would let go. I sobbed until my mouth was parched. Looking around, I noticed the room had thinned considerably. Perhaps the piercing emotions were too close to home.

Finally, an incredible shift occurred. I stopped crying, and the feelings of sadness evaporated. Suddenly, my heart became an antenna attached to a finely tuned radio, and powerful vibrations of overwhelming love danced through my airways. If I looked at a person, I didn't see their physical form, but the greatest feeling of care and compassion for them poured into my heart. Everywhere I looked, I felt love. I wasn't imagining love or thinking of love. I felt deep love. However, it didn't only come from the people—everything exuded love: the floor, the ceiling, the tables, the lamps. The mystics call it *the unity*. Everything was One, His love without separation felt in all of existence. It was the most wondrous feeling. But it wasn't something new.

At eighteen, I had a similar experience. I had been a Christian since age fourteen, and after attending an intense spiritual retreat with the Fellowship of Christian Athletes in Black Mountain, North Carolina I decided that I wanted a direct experience of the Divine. A bible verse suggested that if I were to "pray unceasingly,"[1] a direct connection with God was possible. In the summer of 1974, I vowed to do this. I vowed to pray unceasingly for twenty-four straight hours. It was August in Knoxville, Tennessee, and I was preparing for my upcoming senior high school football season. I awoke and started the continual prayer. At breakfast, I did it silently. I then moved to our front yard, where I was doing some football drills. It was warm but not excessive. I was well hydrated.

About six hours into the prayer, an altered state of consciousness overtook me. Suddenly, I could feel God's love in everything. If I looked at a tree or the grass, I felt love. The sky pulsated with His love. Everything dazzled with His amorous embrace. Even the August air caressed my face lovingly. It was the most intensely beautiful and exhilarating feeling I had ever experienced up to that point in my life. My whole body vibrated with His oneness and love. I remained outside throwing a football through a tire hung from a tree till late afternoon.

I went inside, took a shower, and waited for dinner time. I sat down with my parents around five thirty but didn't tell them what I felt. If they thought I was acting strangely, they didn't say it. After dinner, I moved to be alone in my bedroom. I sat at my desk, continuing to experience the altered reality. Eventually, I lay down on my bed but I couldn't sleep. The vibration was too intense. I lay awake all night feeling the joyous and strange sensation of a scintillating love emanating from everything around me.

In the morning, I avoided people. I once more went outside, but now I sat among the trees in the side yard of our house, continuing to bask in the onslaught of love. By the following evening, I was exhausted. I hadn't slept for thirty-six hours. The intense feelings of love continued to pulse through my body. As I lay down to sleep, I wanted the experience to stop. The vibration scared me. I said a prayer, asking God to remove what was happening.

Introduction

Soon, I fell asleep, and the incredible experience was gone when I woke up in the morning. I was relieved. Oddly, I wasn't the same person I had been before the experience. A window had opened, and I had been given a glimpse of a hidden spiritual world. I searched for a way to regain that experience for the next twenty-two years. I joined an Eastern Religion Self-Realization Fellowship and began meditating regularly, but it wasn't until I turned forty that God answered my prayers. He led me to a Sufi Master, a guide of the love. I pledged to take him as my teacher. And it was during his first visit to my home that I reexperienced the amazing reality of Divine love.

Later that evening, I sat down with this holy man, my Spiritual Guide, and asked him what had happened to me.

"Your heart was being purified. It was a deep opening of your heart. The crying was a release of all the negative emotional experiences built up over a lifetime of sorrow and inner pain. You were given a glimpse of the possibility of a heart that lives in Divine unity." He paused, staring at me intently. "Now, you must continue your journey to your inner heart."

Over the last twenty-five years, I have continued that journey. The mystical Sufis, the great lovers of the Divine, call it *the Path of Love.* This holy man, this Sufi Master, eventually permitted me to teach this path to other people. *Inner Peace Now* is my humble attempt to share nonreligious, heart-opening, and transformative skills with people whose hearts are crying.

Understand that a powerful storm is battering all of us. Hurricane-force winds and waves are pummeling humanity emotionally, psychologically, and physically. The upheaval has precipitated a massive disruption of our lives, and other forces are pounding our psyches: global warming, economic turmoil, systemic racism, and countless other inner and outer conflicts perpetrated on humanity.

We should not lose hope.

Our hearts carry the secrets of profound relief. They have been programmed by the All-Loving, All-Merciful Creator, and The Divine blueprint can be unearthed. We can access and apply the hidden knowledge within our hearts. We don't have to be drowned by the storms of life.

In *Inner Peace Now,* you will learn a unique healing method. Many self-help books claim to be different, but most ask you to shape, change, or undo your thoughts. They work only with the mind. In *Inner Peace Now,* I don't ask you to change your thinking. Instead, methods that work directly at the heart level will be taught. You'll be introduced to a powerful, ancient skill called *The Remembrance*. A simple, easy method for developing a deep heart connection will flood your heart with love and create genuine, lasting change.

The Sufis say that love enters the heart every time a person performs *The Remembrance* (a technique of repeating the Name of the Divine). Such love isn't abstract. It may be invisible to the eye, but it is as real as the electricity that lights our homes. With each practice of *The Remembrance,* an electric current of love flows and nourishes every cell of your human body. It pulsates into the dark and clouded negative emotional centers of our hearts. It cleans and purifies the deep aching and anguish that lies within us. Eventually, such *Remembrance* of love transforms our hearts.

Introduction

As someone who has traveled that inner healing journey and is still traveling its road, I ask you to join me. Through the real story of one of my healing patients, Gabriel Aziz, you'll experience one man's story of transformation.

You wouldn't be reading these words if the All-Loving, All-Merciful hadn't brought you here. Take your chance. Continue reading. Put one foot in front of the other and begin walking. The door is open. The experience of a lifetime awaits.

Peace, love, and blessings.
Dr. Kirk Laman, the Wholehearted Cardiologist.

1

DANCING IN THE STORM

*Not all storms come to disrupt your life.
Some come to clear your path.*
—PAULO COELHO

The emotional storm hammered Gabriel in a way he never thought possible. Gale force winds of fear and anxiety perpetuated by the COVID-19 pandemic had brought the whole world *and him specifically* to their knees in a matter of weeks.

"Why is this happening?" he said to himself, holding his face in his hands. "How could this be happening to me?"

It was two a.m. The sky was black. Ominous clouds of a threatening tropical storm filled the Florida sky. The rain hadn't started, but it would come. The TV news predicted heavy rains would pound the coast and bring a barrage of flash flooding.

Gabriel Aziz perched on the edge of his bed. He nervously brushed a hand through his thickly coiled black hair. He was thirty-four and proud of his level of physical fitness, honed by regular workouts. Intensity coursed through his being and flashed across his angular face. He was a thoughtful and kind man, but, sometimes, his judging of people overtook his compassion. You knew where you stood with Gabriel. He didn't smile in your face with subterfuge. If he didn't like you, you felt his heat.

Gabriel had never been afraid of the weather. Growing up in Morocco, near the desert, he was used to nature's ferocity. Indeed, the menacing storm was the least of his worries. For the last few weeks, severe chest pain had racked his mid- to upper chest. It felt like a spear was being jabbed over and over deep into his chest muscles. The lancinating thunderbolts incapacitated him. The agony propagated up his neck and into his temples, causing massive headaches.

Still, as bad as his chest felt, the overwhelming fear and anxiety were worse. They were paralyzing. As a child, he had experienced fear. Fear came to him hard and fast in the form of his father's strong right hand. Whenever he had done something that displeased his father, Omar—bad grades, playing too late at night in the street, ignoring his chores, anything—he feared the pain of his father's strong right arm administering a beating with his thick, black leather belt. Fear of a whipping was a known and measured fear. When he didn't get good marks in school, his father would scream at him, slap him in the face, and tell him, "You'll never amount to anything."

Now, his fear was different. It swept in like a tidal wave, a limitless ocean of crashing of wind and surf. Wave after wave of terrorizing panic flooded his mind. Was he truly sick? Did he have the dreaded coronavirus? Were the cough and chest pain clues that he was starting to die?

The strangest thing was that he had no idea why he felt panicky.

It came out of nowhere like misty foam that materialized on the beach. And then the terror of being alone and completely lost would pound its way through him. In the beginning, the panic surfaced when he watched the horrible death counts from COVID-19 on the television news. The more he watched, the more he began to feel sick. Eventually, his daytime anxiety moved into the night.

He had never had trouble falling or staying asleep. His job at a restaurant as a dishwasher and general kitchen help required lifting heavy crates of dishes for eight to ten hours a day. By the end of the day, he was exhausted. Usually, the moment he came home he collapsed into bed. He never worried about drifting off to sleep. He was out the moment his head hit the pillow.

Now, just thinking about sleeping made him quake with apprehension. Most nights, he would fall asleep, but within an hour, he would jolt awake. Thoughts of death, illness, and isolation haunted him. Cold sweat soaked his sheets, and inexplicable fear gripped him. Soon, electric shocks of chest pain would course through his upper chest. Any movement intensified the shocks. He dared not breathe. All he could do was pray. Over and over, he asked God for relief.

This cycle of chest pain and suffering lasted for what seemed an eternity. In reality, it was only one to two minutes. One to two minutes of torment, then it mysteriously dissipated like thunderous waves being pulled back into the sea. Unfortunately, his fear refused to leave. The incomprehensible dread smothered all rational thought. He called it "drowning from the inside out." He felt so utterly lost and hopeless that he often wished to die. Soon, he became afraid to sleep. His nights disintegrated into endless, fitful, fearful journeys. He only wanted it to stop.

The first time he was significantly afflicted, he went to urgent care. He roused his younger brother Adam out of deep slumber. It was three a.m.

"What's happening?" Adam asked, rubbing his eyes as he pulled on a pair of pants and a shirt.

"I've got severe chest pain," Gabriel explained. "I've got to go to the doctor."

They climbed into their ancient white Toyota Corolla. It rumbled to life, and they shot down the deserted streets. A full moon illuminated the towering storm clouds of the night sky. Gabriel clutched his chest, grimacing as they drove. Each bump sent violent electric shocks through his chest. The excruciating pain only intensified his fear. They came to a rough stop outside an all-night urgent care. The staff ushered him back into a sterile exam room. Antiseptic smells flooded his nostrils. A yawning, sleepy-eyed doctor nonchalantly listened to his story. He poked and prodded Gabriel's ribs and chest roughly. They performed an electrocardiogram, introductory lab work, and a chest X-ray. They told him nothing was wrong. "It is all in your head," the doctor said. The staff sent him home. A few days later, when the chest pains became more intense, he rushed to the ER.

"I think I'm having a heart attack," he said to them.

Further chest X-rays, ECGs, and lab tests all showed nothing.

"It's a musculoskeletal pain," the ER physician finally said. She was a young woman with a thin frame and a narrow set of cool blue eyes. *She's an intern probably*, Gabriel thought, *couldn't be much older than twenty-four or five.* She glanced at his chart and chewed her lip, then said, "I'm sure it's nothing serious." She told him to rest and not to worry and gave him a prescription for full-strength ibuprofen. But Gabriel knew *something* was wrong. Something serious *had* to be wrong. He had never felt this kind of pain. The reassurances of the ER physician and the ibuprofen helped with the pain, but his panic wouldn't subside.

"Why am I anxious and fearful?" he asked himself. He was sitting on his couch at home a few days after his trek to the ER, trying to make sense of things. He didn't know what was happening to him or why. All he knew was that he was fine until the pandemic exploded globally. Like everyone in America, he had fixated on the onslaught of somber news. In the beginning, work was a distraction. Soon, however, as the virus spread across America, he was laid off. Now, his preoccupation with his illness intensified. While staying at home, he did nothing but search the internet nonstop for news of the disease.

Being ill didn't sit well with Gabriel. He had always considered himself strong and unstoppable. He prided himself on being healthy. He didn't smoke or drink. Each week, he converged on the gym, where he ran and lifted weights at least four or five days a week. His ability to work hard and long was something he congratulated himself on. He rarely even caught a cold, much less an actual illness. But now, his mind began fixating on germs, disinfectants, and disease.

Oddly, something much deeper unsettled him. Getting laid off from work was more bruising internally than he had imagined. Indeed, it had fractured something in his mental armor. He had never been out of work. Since his mid-twenties, he had always contributed to his own welfare. He and his brother lived together in an apartment. They shared expenses fifty-fifty. His brother's job working with disadvantaged youth had been deemed essential by the state, and he continued to work. Now, Gabriel had not started receiving his unemployment checks or government stimulus money, and Adam was paying most of the bills.

Being unemployed brought up traumatic memories from childhood for Gabriel. Growing up In Morocco, few jobs existed. Gabriel lived under his father's incessant harping about his inadequacies for several years after high school graduation. To please his father, he attended the Law University in Rabat, the capital of Morocco. But he dropped out after a year because of boredom. Once more, his father's slurs and verbal abuse mounted. Soon, he enrolled in a two-year computer training certificate program. Even though he graduated with honors, no job awaited him. Of course, his father wasn't satisfied.

"You should have been top in your class," his father had scolded.

He'd never forgotten the time when he was a young adult going to take the exam that would allow him to work in hotel management. His father had chosen to go with him on the bus. During the ride, his father began deriding him so loudly that all the passengers from his neighborhood could hear. Gabriel remembered the uneasy looks of pity in their eyes.

"You're worthless. You'll never amount to anything but a beggar in the street."

He remembered looking down to avoid other people's eyes, ashamed and humiliated. Needless to say, he didn't pass the test.

Now, such memories pushed their way forward into his consciousness. He kept thinking. *Why is this happening? How could this be happening to me?*

Gabriel's life was in peril. It was literally being blown apart in a way he couldn't have imagined just a few weeks earlier. Panic, fear, and overwhelming anxiety flooded his life. A storm was raging with no answers or real help.

Gabriel found himself dancing in the wake of this emotional storm. Wildly, uncontrollably, he was pushed and pulled this way and that, twisted helplessly by the storm. He hadn't chosen this dance floor. Covid-19 had unleashed it, but any of life's challenges could have caused the terror gripping Gabriel. It is a storm that most of us face in one way or another. We eventually find ourselves stretched seemingly to the point of being broken by life. We might be racked by a life-threatening severe heart condition or diagnosed with stage four cancer. Perhaps we have suffered the unbearable loss of a spouse or child. Many of us are pushed against a wall because of the loss of our jobs and the financial fear it instills. Others suffer from emotional calamities—overwhelming anxiety, depression, or mental turmoil. Whatever the insult, no one is immune.

So, we must dance. We must weave and gyrate as we're slung from one partner to the next. We search here and there, looking for answers to the questions that have us reeling. Our minds often spin in a dizzying cacophony of voices. They tell us, "Do this." "No, do that." Trapped in this unrelenting storm, it's easy to lose our way. The peace and happiness we so desperately crave appears elusive. We struggle and fight to keep our heads above water. Yet, another path exists that can direct our hearts along the road to inner peace. It is the path of the heart.

In her book *Didn't See That Coming*, Rachel Hollis writes about the sudden upheaval in her life: "Three days into editing this book, my marriage ended. A sixteen-year marriage to the father of my four children, and an eighteen-year relationship with my best friend. The foundation of my life, everything that once was, crumbled between one breath and another."[2]

Life can sting us in this way. Often, it catapults us from a known and comforting stability to a nearly instantaneous "earth moving under your feet" experience in a few seconds. Like a tragic car accident that leaves you damaged for life, caused by something small, seemingly inconsequential. You accidentally look down to check the radio and fail to see a truck that has run the light that you are rapidly approaching. You have no time to react. In a millisecond, the deafening, sick sound of metal upon metal being torn apart blasts your ears. The next thing you know, you wake up in the hospital, wrapped in bandages. You find your life will never be the same.

What about Gabriel's disaster, COVID-19? An invisible virus ravaged the whole world (and Gabriel's life in particular) in just a few weeks. The great nations, with their aircraft carriers, armies, and nuclear weapons, were beaten back into a full retreat, powerless. Economies were decimated. Nation after nation was panic-stricken, rushing headlong into a lockdown of fear and panic.

Perhaps you are just now entering a vortex, caught up in a swirling tornado—divorce, illness, betrayal—gripped by a life crisis so bleak that it makes you question everything in your life, even your will to live.

If your heart is racing and you feel your whole body trembling, don't fear.

At this point, I want to share a secret. It is the most essential secret you will need to navigate a crisis and regain your peace of heart and mind.

The chaos you feel isn't really chaos.

A deep love is moving silently and mercifully within the waters of the hurricane that has seemingly laid waste to your world. It is the guiding hand of the Most-Loving, All-Compassionate Creator of the entire universe.

He is your ultimate Guide, mine, and everyone's.

You may think this is preposterous. Likely, you will reject it out of hand.

"How can such sorrow, misery, and suffering be love?" you ask. "If God is a loving God, how can He allow such agony to befall His creations, including me?" "Can inner and outer turmoil really be seen and lived as love?"

My answer to you is "Yes."

Turmoil can *indeed* be lived as love. We can discern it if we peer deeply into the mystery we call life. But our gaze cannot be superficial. We must take off our regular glasses and lower our heads closer and closer so our faces are nearly scraping the surface of the calamity. We must courageously inhale the fumes of panic and fear, and as they wash over and permeate within our being, we must ask the All-Loving to show us the real truth behind the tragedy. And if we look deeply, more deeply than we have perhaps ever thought possible, we can begin to see past the pain of the outer tragedy and slowly begin to discern the

All-Compassionate's hand, leading and guiding what seems a paradox of misery within.

Indeed, understanding this paradox requires looking with a new eye. We need to throw off the outer eye, the usual way we have grown accustomed to viewing the world, and look with an inner vision.

We must look with the eye of the heart.

What do I mean by this? The eye of the heart?

Most people don't know that our heart also has an eye. Our heart can see, but it looks with unique wisdom. It sees through the lens of love.

How can I explain the lens of love? The lens of love is best described as the eye of the mother. A mother gazes at her child through a lens of unconditional love and compassion. Her love is without depth or limits. It extends, nurtures, and perpetually holds her child. It is inexplicable. She still loves her children even when they fail or misbehave in ways society deems wrong. Our Lord created a mother's love, and His love for His creatures is much greater. The All-Compassionate, All-Loving feeds and cares for all of his creation continually and without interruption. He provides food and sustenance to everyone and everything. His loving eye is on every human being. His eye is also on the trillions of ants, beetles, and other insects. As the Christian song says, "His eye is on the sparrow, and I know He watches me."[3] Another saying that explains His watchfulness and care: "God sees the black ant, on the black rock on a moonless night, and He gives it what it doesn't expect, but what it needs."[4] What this tells us is that the Universally Merciful, the All-Loving Creator looks after His creations.

His overflowing love and care do not only extend to the good and the kind. Even the evilest and most despicable person receives guardianship and love from the Creator. His compassionate eye sees all. It nurtures and gives to everything.

When earth-shattering events shake us to the core and we say, "Why me? Why now?" we must look at the chaos with the eye of our hearts. The loving eye looks at the difficulty tormenting our lives and sees a secret message of opportunity. Turmoil and difficulty are fertile ground for change and growth.

Psychiatrist M Scott Peck, M.D., writes in his book *The Road Less Traveled,* "Life is difficult. This is a great truth, one of the great truths. It is a great truth because once we truly see this truth, we transcend it. Once we truly know that life is difficult—once we truly understand and accept it—then life is no longer difficult. Because once it is accepted, the fact that life is difficult, it no longer matters."[5]

The difficulty we all feel from life's challenging events doesn't have to overpower us. Yes, our lives may have been mangled, torn asunder. Uncertainty, fear, and panic are common reactions. Doubt about our futures can be paralyzing. But all of this is the outer symptom. Remember, "His eye is on the sparrow." The All-Merciful is watching. He will provide for us as He has always provided. But what truly matters, we must ask ourselves, is, What is the All-Loving trying to tell us with this tragic event that is upending our lives?

A greater truth lies beneath the surface. In the early stages of his healing journey Gabriel couldn't see that The All-Loving was trying to show him that we, as human beings, have lost our way. We have veered off course. The compass guiding our lives is pointed in the wrong direction. It is a direction that does not lead to inner peace and contentment. We have drifted away, abandoning the path that leads to love. Our All-Compassionate creator operates through the music of love. His love vibrates within creation in a harmonious melody of connection, inspiration, and caring.

It is a great secret that within the tragedy that befalls us, the All-Loving is calling us, singing to us through His song of love. It is a beautiful, mystifying siren call to return to Him, to return to the One True Thing that will give our hearts and souls what they want and need. He is calling us to start the journey to our inner heart.

Your illness, divorce, or loss may seem like a disaster, but it is a reminder. A potent reminder for all who must live through the peril. Like the rap, rap, rap of a hailstorm, a barrage of brutal, icy reminders designed to wake us up, the All-Loving is asking us to examine our lives and see *where our focus is.* Is our focus outward? Are we preoccupied with *things?* Mesmerized with the *outerness, the dazzle* of material things? Or is our focus inward, searching for *love?*

You see, this is the *way* many personal obstacles come about. We have been taken in and overcome by the glitter of the outer world, the world of self. It is a world of illusion. The All-Merciful is calling because we have forgotten what is essential. A beautiful children's book, *The Little Prince,* tells us that "what is essential is invisible to the eye."[6] Love, love for family, love for our neighbors, and love for the other people of the world are what is essential in life. Love for yourself is also critical. The outer eye cannot see such love. It is indeed invisible to it. Importantly, the heart knows and feels it.

"Hey," you may say, "why do I need this? I am self-sufficient. I have a job and make my own money. I pay my bills. I do what I want when I want."

But are you really independent? That illusion should have been swept away if you've experienced any personal tragedy. The truth is far different. The truth is that we are one virus, one divorce, one health crisis away from a life of difficulty and despair.

Here's a personal story to illustrate this better. A short time ago, I went to see a dermatologist to have an age spot removed from my face. As we talked, I thought of having her check my back. I had no reason to do this. I hadn't seen or felt anything unusual.

I lifted my shirt, and as she examined my back, she said, "Oh, you have a suspicious lesion here."

A tremble of fear ran through my mind.

The dermatologist took a biopsy, and a week later, it came back positive for malignant melanoma. Malignant melanoma is an aggressive, life-threatening form of skin cancer. If not caught early, the outcome can be devastating. I had to wait four weeks and undergo a large incision in my back that left a hole the size of a grapefruit, but the final pathology report came back negative. Thankfully, my tumor was in its earliest stages, and I was cured. But what if that odd thought hadn't been placed in my mind? Because of its location, I never would have seen it. It could have gone unnoticed for years and metastasized throughout my body.

As they say, life can turn on a dime.

I don't mean to scare you or to be negative, but I believe life's problems are necessary. They are a wake-up call to help us examine our preoccupation with self that reigns in our lives—the thoughtlessness that many of us have embraced. We need to peer deeply into our predicaments that have torn apart the fabric of life.

As an example, consider the life cycle of families.

Families used to be close-knit tribes of support, a place to come home to for both parents and child. Unfortunately, in the last fifty years, families have changed. The bond between parents and their children has eroded. Children have become so wrapped up in their own lives that they are oblivious to the needs or desires of their parents. Often, the weakness of that relationship exists for a good reason. So it's not fair to point fingers. But more and more parents feel their children have abandoned them. They see their children only a few times a year, even if they live just a few miles away. It is a text message here or there, but genuine concern has faded into the background.

Another way we have lost our way is that we have not been *grateful*. We have taken for granted the untold gifts showered upon us. Food, clothing, a place to work and live—the very cloth of our society and lives—is a gift from the Most Generous.

Even more importantly, we have been caught up in our material lives and have forgotten our Creator. We have become mindless and move mindlessly through life, scratching the ground for *things*—expensive cars, dazzling houses, and delightful clothes. Unfortunately, most people have neglected to reflect on their Creator. We have abandoned God and embraced the things of the world. When we ask ourselves, as Gabriel Aziz asked, "Why me? Why now?" I would suggest that The Creator is asking us to look deeply within. Have we traveled off the path toward peace, love, mercy, and justice? It's time to change the course of our lives. What disasters and illness can show us is that it's time to reflect upon our lives. It may be time to change how we love and how we are loving.

It is time to begin your journey down *The Path of Love,* if you are willing. As a humble traveler down this path, I find it answers the question of "Why Me? Why Now?"

The All-Loving has allowed the powerful winds of misfortune and tragedy to pummel us. They knock us this way and that. The dance has begun. It has indeed intensified. Interestingly, love is coursing behind these challenges. The question is: "Will we heed the call of the Most Loving?" His song is playing. Listen for it. It is a tender song filled with hope that can bring you peace. Are you willing to start the journey and dance your way deeper into your heart?

2

THE PATH OF LOVE

When you choose to walk on the way of love, You will be filled with love wherever you go in this world. You will find everything beautiful.

—RUMI

The pain that seared Gabriel's chest increased after his second ER visit. The episodes of pain and panic battered him daily. He tried his best to cope by following the advice of friends to get out of the apartment. Often, he would get up early. He moved silently while getting ready to leave, careful not to wake his brother. He prepared his clothes, bike, and water bottle the night before, and he scurried down to the beach on his bicycle. A local beachfront park was located only a few miles from his apartment. In semi-darkness, he rode the streets deep in thought.

Of course, early in the morning, the park was deserted. A local homeless person who had escaped the police rounds often lay in the shadows, hidden by foliage. Gabriel would deposit a few dollars into the shopping cart piled with his ratty possessions. The forlorn man knew of Gabriel's frequent offerings and kept a watchful eye on Gabriel's bike. Gabriel would park not far from the man, lock his bike, and go to the water's edge. He generally took off running briskly, pushing himself into the wind. He would jog down the beach for nearly an hour. The scent of the ocean and the sound of the waves calmed him as they cascaded to shore. Once tired, he strolled more leisurely back to where he had left his bike. He would sit quietly and watch the seagulls fluttering about in the wind. The feel of the sand, sticky and wet between his toes, was comforting. Yet, his mind wouldn't let him escape into a book or relax completely. Eventually, he'd return to his apartment. He tried not to watch the awful talking heads on the news, but the internet on his cell phone wasn't much better.

One Wednesday, after a couple of weeks of trying to deal with his suffering using only ibuprofen, he awoke with severe anxiety. The spasms of fear and electric shocks of pain in his chest would not abate.

"What is going on?" he said to himself after being racked with another attack. Visions of death and abandonment clouded his thinking. He couldn't cope with it any longer. He finally decided to call his family physician, hoping she could provide some relief. But her office was shut down. He spoke to the doctor on call. When Gabriel mentioned he was having chest pain, the physician directed him back to the ER. After sitting at home for a couple of hours debating with himself about whether to go to the emergency room again, he started having even more intense chest pain. With panic bubbling up inside, he once again asked his brother to drive him to the ER. It was seven-thirty in the evening when he pushed his way through the automatic doors of the ER and took his place in line.

He squirmed impatiently, shifting from one foot to the other, as he stood on the yellow lettering painted on the floor, with nearby signs saying, "Please stand six feet apart." After thirty minutes in pre-triage, a voice called him to a small window.

"So, you don't have a fever?" the bored ER triage nurse said after taking his name and birthdate. She wore an N-95 mask, a see-through plastic face shield, and green full-body protective gear. Everything was invisible except for her eyes. They were dark brown, like the glimmer of hair that protruded slightly from the top of her facial barrier. Gabriel glanced through the door to the left. Overhead, fluorescent lights flickered in the triage area that was packed with people of all ages. She tapped her clipboard absentmindedly with her pen. Gabriel glanced down at her numbered list. He could see the number twenty-five with names of various conditions—shortness of breath, fever, a fractured arm, and multiple people with possible COVID-19 infections. He realized that only the sickest patients could enter through the main ER doors.

"No, but I have incredible pain. I'm sure I'm having some heart condition," he said. "I've got a cough too. It's been going on for weeks. I've also been short of breath."

"It's here again," he said, as his body contorted in pain. He grimaced, clutching his upper chest. The debilitating spasm left sweat pouring down his face.

"I know this is difficult. But you're thirty-four years old," she said with a little shake of her head. "Your chest pain is worse when you take a deep breath, right?"

He nodded.

"The chances of you having a major heart condition are remote. You don't have a fever. We only have Covid tests for people with a fever." She started to wave him away

"My breathing is getting worse," he said.

She turned and peered back at him. She cocked her head sideways, thinking for a moment. "Okay, let me talk to the doctor and see if we can get you in." She swiped her badge on the keypad and disappeared through another set of large automatic doors. A few minutes later, she was back. She motioned him forward. Inside, a female medical assistant directed him to an examining room. He was given a gown and told to undress. Shortly, she returned and placed his clothes in a large green plastic bag with the hospital's logo on it. She put it on a small metal nightstand. Once more, he was hooked up to a heart monitor that constantly made annoying beeping sounds. A few moments later, the emergency room physician, a large, chubby, African American doctor in full protective gear, entered the room. He interviewed and examined Gabriel. He poked Gabriel's chest, making him wince.

"Humm," the doctor said, nodding his head. He went to the computer and began typing. "I'm going to order a few tests," he said and left the room. After fifteen minutes, the laboratory people came and drained tube after tube of blood from his arm.

"Why do you need so much blood?" he asked, looking down at all the glass tubes.

A short woman, faceless behind her protective gear, shrugged her shoulders. "It's what we do. The doctor ordered the tests. I don't ask why." Next, they attached him to an electrocardiogram, and later he was wheeled on a gurney to get an X-ray of his chest.

Standing up against the cold X-ray plate made him tremble with pain. Without a word, they wheeled him back to his room.

Gabriel lay alone in the bed. The separation from his brother, who was required to wait outside due to Covid protocols, was the most difficult part of the ER visit. Gabriel stared up at the heart monitor. His heart was galloping uncontrollably at one hundred twenty-five beats a minute. Each beat thumped harder and harder. His breath became labored. Soon, the electric shocks of pain began seizing his chest.

Am I going to die all alone? he thought. He screamed for the nurse. No one came. He screamed a second and then a third time. Finally, after what seemed an eternity, a very young nurse entered the room.

"It's my chest," he said through clenched teeth. "The pain is unbearable."

She looked up at the monitor, listened to his chest, and quickly left the room. In less than a minute, an older nurse entered with the young nurse. She pulled up his medical chart on the computer and reviewed his tests. She moved close to him and placed her hand on his lower ribs.

"Does this hurt?" she asked as she squeezed his chest.

"Yes," he said, recoiling quickly. "That's it. That makes it worse."

"I see," she said, nodding her head. "We're going to get you something for the pain." Casually, she motioned for the other nurse, and they left the room. After a few minutes, she returned with a syringe of clear liquid in her hand. She lifted his IV port. "I'm going to give you something to relax," she said.

"Relax? I've got chest pain," he said.

"Yes, I know, but the doctor thinks it's anxiety," she said. With a quick push, she emptied the contents of the syringe into the IV. She dialed new settings into the IV infusion pump, flushing the liquid into his body. "You should feel better soon." She pulled the curtains that hung from the ceiling around his bed and left the room.

Humph, I know it's not anxiety, he thought. *I've got real chest pain. It can't be anxiety.* Within a few minutes, Gabriel could feel the medicine begin to kick in. A floating, mellow feeling seeped over him.

Gabriel stayed in the emergency room for three more hours. Finally, the African American doctor returned to his room with another nurse.

"All your tests are back, and everything is normal. We checked your electrocardiograms and cardiac enzymes. We ruled out a heart attack. Your chest X-ray shows a normal heart size, and you don't have pneumonia. Nothing serious is going on. I think you are having panic attacks," he said.

"Listen, doctor," Gabriel said, "my chest pain is real. It's not a panic attack. "

The physician nodded his head slowly. "Yes, I'm sure it's real, but sometimes panic attacks can cause real pain. It can seem just like a heart attack. But we've checked you out. You're not having a heart attack. You're young, and the chances of you having a heart attack with normal enzymes and electrocardiogram are remote. We are discharging you and suggest you follow up with your family physician."

The Path of Love

"My family physician's office is closed. What will I do until I can get in to see her?" he asked. "The ibuprofen isn't working."

The physician cocked his head to the right, thinking for a few seconds.

"Okay, here's what I am going to do. I'm going to give you ten tablets of a medication called Tramadol. It's a mild pain reliever. I'm also going to give you a prescription for a mild anti-anxiety medication. This will get you through until you can see your PCP. I'll also give you a psychologist's name and phone number. I think you should see her. It could help." He turned to the nurse. "I'll fill out his discharge orders." With that, he exited the room.

"Okay, Mr. Aziz," she said. "I'll be back with some paperwork shortly." She quickly exited the room as well.

Twenty minutes later, Gabriel walked carefully out of the ER. He had been in the ER for four and a half hours. He trudged over to the black Toyota Corolla. His brother was sitting at the wheel, tapping his hands to music on the radio.

"Well, what happened?" his brother asked after he opened the door and dropped into the passenger seat.

"They think it's all in my head," he said. "They gave me some different pain pills, something for anxiety, and they want me to see a psychotherapist."

His brother thought for a few seconds, then said, "I think it's time you tried something different." said

Fear and anguish are common feelings when the storms of life pelt people. Trepidation overwhelms people. They shake with apprehension about an unknown future. Unresolved wounds they had previously repressed, wounds of recrimination, self-doubt,

31

and self-loathing often resurface. Others grieve for the carefree life they used to know. Life before any tragedy seems like an innocent time. Looking back, it usually appeared stable and secure. Once a storm overtakes us, life is a jumbled mess of uncertainty.

What we need to understand is that such feelings are common. It's important not to lose hope. Solace can be found. The teachings I am about to share with you can be a balm for your wounds. The healing you seek is within your grasp. Open your heart and let go of the doubts and beliefs hindering your movement forward. Look deep with the eye of your heart. What you are searching for can be found inside you. Your heart is the key to ridding your life of panic, fear, and paralysis. The journey you need to take is the journey toward inner peace.

I received a phone call from a dear friend, Gabriel's sister, shortly after his second visit to the emergency room. She inquired about my willingness to work with Gabriel regarding his emotional problems. I am a physician of the heart and a cardiologist, and I practice typical cardiology. I see patients who have diseases of the physical heart. However, quite commonly, in practicing traditional cardiology, I find that many of what are called *physical illnesses* have their beginnings in emotional and psychological trauma. The psychological illness comes first, then the physical illness follows. The interaction between mind, body, and what can be called *spirit or soul* has been recognized and documented in the traditional cardiac research literature. Cardiac conditions that produce actual physical illness are not rare; they are quite common.

One malady that frequently rears its ugly head is called *Stress*

Cardiomyopathy. It is a condition in which a person's heart becomes suddenly weakened due to overwhelming stress. Often, it appears that the person is having a heart attack. Electrocardiographic changes, shortness of breath, and abnormal cardiac enzyme release occur, mimicking an Acute Coronary Syndrome. The person will often undergo a cardiac catheterization to rule out a coronary artery occlusion. A plastic tube will be inserted in the artery of the wrist or leg and advanced to the heart. The coronary arteries will be injected with dye and evaluated. Their heart arteries will be normal, showing no cholesterol blockages. However, their heart muscle will be damaged in a peculiar pattern resembling a Japanese octopus trapping pot called a *Takutsubo*.[7] The upper portion of their heart muscle will be normal, and the apex or tip of the heart will be severely weakened.

Another common cardiac problem arising from fear and stress is a racing heart. Once or twice a week, patients crippled with anxiety show up as new patients in my office suffering from uncontrollable tachycardias. They have abnormal heart rhythms that are real. Their hearts may be speeding at one hundred fifty, one hundred sixty, or even two hundred beats a minute. Shortness of breath overtakes them, and like Gabriel, their chest frequently aches. They may experience lightheadedness, and some of them even collapse unconscious on the floor. Through traditional cardiac testing—an ultrasound of the heart, a stress test, or wearing a cardiac rhythm monitor—we determine if they have structural heart disease or something physically wrong with their hearts. Medications are frequently administered to slow the racing heart rhythm and stop the episodes of tachycardia hindering their lives. Unfortunately, as a traditional cardiologist, I don't often address their psychological issues. I leave that up to their family physician and psychologist.

Psychological issues can even have more serious cardiac consequences. Although it is relatively uncommon, a person can die suddenly from psychological trauma. Research has shown that many patients have dropped dead instantly after hearing horrific news such as about the World Trade Center attacks. Unexpected phone calls with the shocking news of a loved one dying can be the catalyst for a condition called Sudden Cardiac Death (SCD). The person dies nearly instantaneously after learning damaging psychic news. Conditions such as being car-jacked or witnessing a murder can provoke SCD. In addition, outbursts of profound anger can induce Sudden Cardiac Death.[8]

My education as a traditional heart doctor enables me to understand and treat the cardiac ramifications of psychological and emotional illness. I've also had special training in helping people heal their inner or spiritual heart. I completed two years of post-graduate training at the University of Spirituality and Sufism in Northern California. I was trained as a spiritual counselor and healer, employing a unique form of therapy that works directly at the heart level. It is based on Sufism, an ancient spiritual discipline known as *Tasawuf*, the way of the wool. The Sufis are the great lovers of the All-Mighty, The-One. Their creed is love, love, and more love. Sufi spiritual techniques are illuminating in their ability to help a person expand and connect deeply to their own heart. A deep heart connection is essential for true emotional and psychological healing and well-being.

The Path of Love

The best-known practical example of Sufi knowledge are the poems and writings of Jalaluddin Rumi. Rumi is one of the poets most often quoted in the Western world. His book, *Mathnawi*, written in the 1200s, is one of the most influential works of Sufism. Understanding and incorporating the Sufi teachings, as illustrated by Rumi, can lift a student out of the realm of superficial loving and propel their heart on the journey to limitless, indescribable love. It is a love that the mind cannot comprehend but can only be contained by the heart of the faithful lover of the All-Mighty.[9]

During my three years of post-graduate education, I was propelled into the orbit of a Sufi Master, Shaykh Muhammad Said ar-Rafa'i (1935-2015). He was a grandfatherly figure with an entrancing smile and boundless compassion. A giant in his field. Muhammad al-Jamal was a true Sufi Master with penetrating insight. He was known as *The Guide of the peace, love, and mercy*. My experience was that he genuinely was "love walking in a human body." Everything about him oozed love. Just being in his presence was intoxicating.

Muhammad al-Jamal was once the head of the Higher Sufi Council of Jerusalem and the Holy Lands. In an outward sense, he was a famous religious figure. When Pope John Paul II came to Jerusalem in 2000 to promote religious tolerance, Shaykh Muhammad was one of the leaders who met with him.

On an inner level, he was a man who guided his students from the gross outer world to the inner subtle world of the heart. For over twenty years, I trained under his watchful eye. I learned a form of a heart healing technique called spiritual healing, which is a profound method that allows a practitioner to guide a person deeply into their heart. The method is quick and highly effective for discovering the underlying psychological issues that have traumatized a person. Quite often, two or three sessions can be the equivalent of years of traditional counseling. During my years with Muhammad al-Jamal, he conferred on me the title of *Master Sufi Healer and Master Sufi Teacher*, and he permitted me to guide students down the Sufi *Path of Love*.

Achieving mastery in a field is different from taking a weekend course. In his book *Outliers*, Malcolm Gladwell talks about the 10,000-hour rule.[10] He contends that no one achieves mastery in any field, whether it be the sport of tennis, playing the violin, the field of medicine, or being a healer, without putting in at least 10,000 hours of training. Being honored with the title of *Master Sufi Healer and Master Sufi Teacher* is no different. To earn such a title exceeded 10,000 hours of contemplation, reflection, study, and training. And I must be honest and humble here by saying I don't consider myself a Master. I would not call myself a Master Teacher or Healer. Like everyone who is The All-Mighty's beloved, I am a beloved of the Divine. I share the message of *The Path of Love* with those interested in ridding their hearts of the panic, fear, and paralysis that is making their lives miserable.

In these Sufi healing sessions, we don't attempt to change a person's religion or impose our own spiritual beliefs upon them. In the past, I have successfully worked with Catholics, Protestants, Jews, Hindus, and people practicing a Native American spiritual tradition. Our goal is not to change people's beliefs but to help them heal their inner hearts.

After talking with Gabriel's sister about his predicament, I agreed

The Path of Love

to try to help him. Two days later, he called, and after speaking with him for ten minutes, it became clear what was troubling him. We arranged to have an in-depth healing session the next day. The spiritual healing I employ is similar in some ways to talk therapy. And, often, it can be accomplished over the phone.

What is different is that the healer, emptied of a focus on his/herself, concentrates on the subject's heart. A therapist trained in these methods opens their own heart and fills it with love. They surround the client's heart with their full-hearted presence. It is a difficult concept to grasp or even believe. An analogy is a magnetic field generated by an MRI. When you step into the magnetic field of an MRI machine, a physical transformation happens within the body's cells that produce an actual physical image. We can't see that field, but we know its presence. Anyone walking into that invisible magnetic space with a piece of metal in their pocket has experienced the magnetic pull of the unseen field.

In addition, studies of quantum physics have shown that even a person's observation can alter the force field of subatomic particles shot at a target.[11] Psychological intention can change the beam of particles toward a person who psychically attempts to influence that field. This may seem like voodoo, but it has been scientifically proven. Further studies have shown that every person's body emits an electromagnetic field that projects outside their physical body. This electromagnetic field interacts with other people's fields when we come in proximity.

Similarly, we have all had the experience of talking on the phone with someone and sensing their emotional state. Whether it's the quality of their voice or other subtle clues, we can get a psychological perception of what is going on at an inner level. Heart-centered Sufi healing methods, like psychotherapy, allow us to interpret what is happening at the person's emotional level.

Gabriel called on a Saturday morning via *WhatsApp*. I asked him to assume a comfortable position. He complied and turned on his camera so I could see his face. We shared a few pleasantries while I studied him.

He looked tired. Dark circles, closely spaced, ringed his eyes. Thick stubble made his face seem like it lay in shadows, although the light in the room was delicate. His expression was pained and panicky, like a spring wound too tightly, and his manner suggested the spring was capable of violently letting go. I also sensed that he was wary. Much later, he told me he had serious doubts about what our sessions could accomplish.

"I thought just my physical heart was having problems," he would tell me. "I had no idea about the depth of the work or what lay beneath the surface of my heart."

I suggested it would work best if he closed his eyes. Next, we used breathing techniques designed to deepen his relaxation. I watched the pained, anxious expression on his face soften as we completed the breathing.

"What I would like you to do now," I said, "is to bring all your focus and attention into your heart region. It's that area just to the lower left of your breastbone. You can place your right hand over your heart if you want." I watched as he did this.

The Sufi techniques for opening and healing the heart require people to make a deep connection, which is often a foreign experience. Most people live their whole lives with hearts

The Path of Love

that are closed or shielded. They are not aware that powerful negative emotional experiences accumulated from a lifetime of psychological suffering and trauma have been locked within their hearts.

"Now, I would like you to focus all your attention on your heart region," I said to Gabriel. "Imagine your attention focused three inches below your right hand within the area where your heart resides. Keep all your focus on this region, and imagine you can feel your heart muscle."

I then had Gabriel begin performing *The Remembrance*.

What is *The Remembrance*? And what are we remembering? *The Remembrance* is a sacred word for God that contains the "Ahhh" sound. Even people who are not religious can say, "Ahhh." It is the primordial sound that all humans make when they feel deeply relaxed. It is a universal sound that rarely needs explanation and transcends all cultures.

My Sufi teacher once said that it is the first word a baby cries when pushed out of the womb. It is a cry of Ahhh. He said the baby's squall isn't a scream of agony. It is a call to their Creator wanting to return. We say, Ahhhh, or we can say, Yaaahwayyy, Jehovaaah, or Allaaaah. If we call to the Divine with the intent of returning to His Light, then the Ahhh sound will fill our hearts.

The bestselling self-help author Wayne Dyer, Ph.D., has published information and audio programs based on using this Divine Name as a form of healing.[12] Remembrance means remembering the All-Loving, the All-Merciful Creator. It is our call to this Divine entity. It is also our return. When we perform *The Remembrance*, we are returning to our source. We are

39

reconnecting to the Divine light that lives inside our hearts. Our *Remembrance* is the return back to our heart

Indeed, *The Remembrance* is much more. The Sufis say *The Remembrance* is the electricity of the All-Loving, All-Caring. They suggest it is the transformational electricity of love. When a person takes a deep breath and verbalizes "Ahhhh," and lets that sound flow deeply into their heart, love enters the heart, and with each heartbeat, this love flows to every cell of the body.

The Remembrance is the hidden magic of existence. When a person sits down, concentrates, and invokes the sound of *The Remembrance,* their heart begins to vibrate. Their chest expands, and calmness floods the psyche. Practicing *The Remembrance* is a natural experience. (See the Appendix for instructions on performing *The Remembrance*.) It's much easier than meditation and more potent than any energy healing. I know this because I previously practiced an Eastern religion for nearly twenty years and utilized its traditional meditative techniques of Om, Hong Song, and Kriya Yoga. I have also explored energy healing methods and have been worked on by energy healers. Of course, every person's experience of different healing modalities is unique. My opinion is only my opinion. It's not my intent to denigrate other types of healing. *The Remembrance* works best for me after exposure to transcendental meditation (TM), mindfulness meditation, Reiki healing, and direct energy techniques. I find it simple and highly organic. Continually utilizing *The Remembrance* enlivens the body and captivates and transforms our psyches. The dedicated practice of *The Remembrance cures many emotional illnesses.*

Based on Gabriel's religious inclination, he wished to use a word for God that he felt comfortable with. He shared the word with me, and I asked him to begin repeating the word out loud. Words can be like music. They carry a particular tone and vibratory quality. We have all seen the example of a person who can sing a particular pitch that can break a glass. *The Remembrance* has such a tonal quality. If you place your hand upon your chest and repeat *The Remembrance*, you can feel your chest and heart region vibrate.

Gabriel performed *The Remembrance* for a few minutes. His breath smoothed out, and his voice carried a more relaxed timbre.

"Now, what are you feeling in your heart?" I asked him. "What is your inner awareness?"

"I don't feel anything," he said.

It is common for people not to be aware of the feelings inside their hearts when they first start doing healing sessions or *Remembrance*. When a heart is closed, we can think of it as an asleep heart. It can take some time to wake a heart accustomed to slumber.

"Keep your attention at the heart level. See if you can feel your heart beating," I said. I took him back to *The Remembrance*. *The Remembrance* is the opener of the heart. The Sufis say that love flows into the heart whenever someone repeats a sacred name for God. The Most-Generous' love is carried on His Name. If a person repeats the Name repeatedly, more and more love spreads through the heart. A virtual river of love washes the heart of a person's sadness, pain, and difficulty. It is like taking a cloth filled with impurities down to the river. A person holds the fabric in the water, and the water cleans the cloth.

"Do you feel any emotions coursing inside your heart, or do you see any pictures?" I asked.

"I still don't feel anything," he said. His breathing quickened. "The pain is starting."

I stared intently at his face and body posture. Something was indeed happening. Tension was creeping from his chin upwards to his hairline. His arms and legs had a slight tremor.

"Stay with the heart. Keep with *The Remembrance*," I said. "It's normal not to be able to feel anything in the beginning. Let *The Remembrance* of the Name go directly into the pain."

I listened to his voice as he repeated the Name over and over. The tension in his body began to settle down, and his breathing once more slowed. "I want you to focus on the area of pain and let your consciousness go into the painful area. What do you feel there?" I asked. A quizzical look flashed across his face.

"I feel some fear and see a picture," he said. His eyes narrowed as if he was staring into the distance. "I see a little boy," he said. "It's me. I must be three or four years old. I'm with my mother, and I'm holding her hand. We are standing in the marketplace. It's the old marketplace, the *Souk*, in downtown Rabat, Morocco. It's gigantic."

I had been to the *Souk* in the capital city of Morocco. It's an expansive open-air market with hundreds of vendors. The sellers are packed together nearly on top of each other. The exotic smells of strange spices and cooked meat from chickens and lamb push into the senses. Screams and pleas from the vendors to "Look at this," "Mister, buy this" fill the air. Everyone is pressed and shoved together, making the whole experience feel unruly and chaotic. It's a jarring experience for an adult. I can't imagine what it would feel like to a child.

"Everyone is next to each other," Gabriel said. "It's so crowded. The people are pushing."

A look of concern tightened his face. His voice became tense and staccato. "A man is between us. He's pulling us apart. I can't feel my mother's hand. I can't feel it. She's not next to me. Too many people, too much confusion. I can't see her. I can't feel her... She's gone. I'm alone." A soft sob began to come from deep within his throat. Tears formed at the corners of his eyes. "I'm all alone."

"It's okay," I said. "Let's go back to *The Remembrance*. Say your word for God. Put it inside the pain and feelings of loneliness."

Gabriel began chanting the Name of God. Soon, the "Ahhh" sound was visibly vibrating his chest. His voice was loud and sometimes cracked with sadness and tears. We continued like this for some time until the pain and sorrow had passed.

I watched as his body posture calmed.

"Now, I want you to do something for me," I said. "I want you to keep your focus on your heart and let your consciousness move even more deeply within your heart. And I want you to ask your heart or your Creator, whatever makes you feel more comfortable, 'How do these pictures from the market relate to the panic and pain that I feel? What is the teaching from these images?'"

"Say the words silently," I said. "Just ask your heart the question," I explained.

Many people trained in Sufi techniques have an intuition of the pictures arising inside their client's hearts. The pictures often contain short, emotional movies of past experiences of trauma. The healer's job is to open their own heart, bringing love within themselves, and then emotionally surround the client with their expanded heart, much like a person would hug someone. No touching ensues since we do it over the phone. But even when performed in person, therapists don't need to touch the client to affect their heart.

Of course, this might seem preposterous to people who have never done it. Still, as explained earlier, scientific research in quantum physics has demonstrated that it is possible to interact and influence objects through psychic intention without physically touching them.[13]

Gabriel did as I requested. He continued to explore his heart, searching for the significance of his surfacing memories. To facilitate his process, I began softly repeating *The Remembrance* out loud. Like a vibrational beat of the music, the "Ahhh" sound penetrated his heart region. After a moment, I stopped verbally toning *The Remembrance* and observed him. After a few moments of silence, emotion again splashed across his face. "Are you getting anything?" I asked. "Do you have any awareness of a link between your experience in the giant market and the panic and pain you feel?"

"Yes, something is coming," he said. I waited. His brow furrowed, and the corners of his lips thickened. I could see he was concentrating.

"It's like staring into a fog. Panic and fear are circling within the mist. And there's something else. Mixed inside is a feeling of loss—of something missing. I can't see it. It's not visible, but I feel it."

"Stay with this," I said. "Let yourself move deeper into it. Imagine you are descending into fear and panic. Once more, call your Creator or ask the wisdom of your heart, 'How do these pictures from the market relate to the panic and pain I feel? What is the teaching from these images?'

Gabriel didn't say anything. I continued to vocalize the comforting sounds of *The Remembrance*. His posture relaxed, and a peaceful expression graced his face.

"It has something to do with my time in Italy," he said. "I was in Italy for nine months with a European visa issued from The Netherlands. I had taken a job with a Moroccan family and was told it was to help as a gardener. After I dropped out of the University of Rabat's law program and finished my computer certificate, I first went to the Netherlands on a study visa for further computer training. I spoke French, English, and Moroccan, but learning Dutch was difficult. I had come to Europe to become a citizen and to make money for my family, who were struggling financially in Morocco.

"I had Moroccan friends in Italy. They assured me I could become a citizen quickly if I came to Italy. When I arrived, I found out that the family didn't have a position for a gardener. They wanted me to help take care of their daughter, who was sixteen years old and had mental illness." When he said the last words, his body tensed. His hands began quivering slightly. He paused.

"Yes, go on," I said.

"I was to watch her and keep her company. They only gave me a few euros a week for pay, and I had just a cot inside a tiny room to sleep in. They kept her confined in her bedroom. They locked the door and wouldn't let her out. During the day, I had to stay inside the bedroom with her. I remember the room walls were painted a stark white, and the paint was peeling. The furniture was old and smelled stale. A tiny window let in the faintest amount of light."

"She was crazy, literally crazy. She would hear voices and scream at spirits she imagined were in the room. I tried to keep her calm. I told her, 'No spirits are here.' But she wouldn't listen. I couldn't handle it, but they made me continue the job. They told me I couldn't go back to the Netherlands. My visa had expired. They held me like a prisoner. I had no money. I felt afraid and alone. In just a few weeks, I started having panic attacks. I began thinking I was going to be crazy. Finally, I called my sister, who was living in Amsterdam, and she drove for sixteen hours straight from Holland to Italy. My visa for the Netherlands had expired. She snuck me out of Italy to live in the Netherlands. I became an illegal."

Gabriel's last sentence rushed out quickly and unevenly. His eyelids flickered wildly. The experience was distressing.

"So, how does this relate to your pain and fear now?" I asked.

His eyes squinted tightly. "I see it now. It's like the fog is lifting. It's the same fear. COVID-19 has made me afraid like before. It's like I'm back in Italy. I'm a prisoner to things I can't control. I'm powerless." A heavy breath escaped from his chest. The tension that had been building inside his body began to dissipate. A sigh escaped his lips.

"Good," I said, "We're getting somewhere."

We concluded the session. I asked him to sit upright.

"How do you feel?" I asked. His face was flushed, and I could see that it still expressed some apprehension.

"I don't understand how what happened to me in Italy would be related to what I'm going through now," he said. "They are completely different situations. I have money in the bank. I'm a U.S. citizen. I'm not a prisoner." He shook his head from side to side.

Then he continued. "I remember that room in Italy so well. It was at the very top of a four-story house. We had to climb these rickety stairs. Each step made a squeak like an animal in pain. The room had this morbid smell of sweat and urine. They locked the door on us during the day so the girl wouldn't run away. The room didn't have a bathroom. They made her relieve herself in a pee pot that we pushed into the corner. I'd put a sheet over her for privacy. When she'd freak out about the spirits, she'd fly about the room and knock over the pot. The stench was horrible. I'll never forget that smell. But I still don't understand what this has to do with the chest pain and anxiety I feel now. Everything is different."

"We are going to get to that," I assured him. You've achieved a significant milestone here. You've *become aware* that something is troubling your heart. Before, you had no idea why you felt anxious or why you were having chest pains. The pieces are going to come together. This is good. We'll see what we uncover in the next session.

I had him mentally review what we had discovered that day. I asked him to start a journal to document the progression of his healing. He was to do *The Remembrance* each morning and night, and as he reflected on his life, he was to write down any feelings or revelations. I stressed to him the importance of this type of self-healing. We made plans to meet a week later.

The *Path of Love* is a framework for overcoming our hearts' anxiety, fear, and emotional upheaval. The first step is *awareness*. We need to become aware that something is amiss in our lives. Gabriel had started the process. He had sought help. Now he was learning that a deep heart connection was essential for the healing he desired and the key to living an abundant, fulfilled life. In his first heart healing session, he had uncovered one piece of the trauma puzzle that was making him anxious. Here lies the difference between the *Path of Love* and traditional psychological thinking. Conventional Western medicine believes emotional injury and traumas are held as memories inside the brain.

The people who follow *The Path of Love* think differently. We believe that our hearts hold this emotional injury through picture movies. Yes, painful memories also reside within the brain's memory centers. Emotional pain is the heart connected to the brain through memory, but we believe the heart is the coordinating center for this type of injury. Scientific research in the last decade has led credence to this belief. A groundbreaking scientific study from the HeartMath Institute has validated the Sufi understanding of emotional trauma.[14] They have documented the existence of powerful nervous centers that reside within the chest and encircle the heart. In response to psychological injury, these plexuses of thousands of neurons are activated before the brain's limbic system.

Our understanding is that psychological wounds are held as pictures, emotional movies that penetrate and enwrap the emotional/spiritual/soulful heart. A simple understanding is to see them as veils or coverings over the inner heart. The Sufi knowledge says that a person is born with a pure and unblemished heart from the pain and trauma of life. Within the heart lies *The Divine Light*. The human soul carries and contains this Light. It is a light of peace, love, mercy, truth, and joy. The love that every human being experiences, whether it is the love of themselves, family, friends, animals, or any activity that gives them joy, springs from this Divine Light. It is the source of everything good and wholesome in the human experience. It is what unites communities, races, and cultures—the light of the All-Merciful lives within us. We are not God or the light of God but a reflection of this light. God is the limitless ocean, and we are the waves. However, the waves and the ocean are inseparable.

A dark veil grows within their heart whenever a person's psyche is bruised, and they respond with feelings of anger or hatred; other negative emotions and actions such as arrogance, malice, envy, stinginess, conceit, lying, backbiting, slander, and other unrighteous acts can also accumulate as veils. These veils cover the Light of The Divine, preventing people from feeling and connecting to their true nature. The veils restrict the flow of love and enable fear, anxiety, and panic to overtake a person.

Dark veils lead to blindness in the heart. I said earlier that our hearts can see. They have an eye. It is the eye of love. A person cannot see with the eye of the heart when their heart is shrouded with dark veils. The heart's eye is clouded. Of course, they laugh. They live and experience life, but it is an existence turned outward toward the material side of life. Rarely do they grasp and experience the true wonder and rapture of a heart whose veils have been lifted. The *Path of Love* demands that we take a new journey. It asks us to travel fearlessly into our hearts. The first requirement is to be aware of what causes the veils. Ultimately, the goal is to open *the door to our hearts* and travel deep into our eternal spirit.

A mighty, unrelenting wind was blowing into Gabriel's life. It is the same staunch wind that blasts into the hearts of all people who are suffering. The wind is strong. It pushes people in unwanted ways. Fear may burden them. Gale-force winds of anxiety and dread may shake their whole being. Indeed, they may have psychological paralysis that overwhelms them. But it's essential to make this expedition to the heart. At first, it may seem like a scary journey. The troubles and tribulations of life have unleashed a typhoon of panic and fear. Thankfully, we need not fear.

Previously, a woman from Virginia contacted me who was suffering from severe emotional problems. She had been told that my healing work could help her emotional sorrow. We talked on the phone for thirty or forty minutes, and she seemed fine. However, once we started the session and she began seeing traumatic pictures from her childhood, she didn't want to continue. I tried to convince her that issues that troubled her heart could be a form of guidance, but the experience was too much. She wasn't willing to reflect deeply on the storm sweeping her life.

These powerful forces are not the winds of tragedy and destruction. The currents don't have to carry malfeasance. If we can look with a deep eye and peer with the eye of the heart, our vision will see the wind of love. The wind is a strong guide that will take you to a place that will give your heart rest.

Every human being's heart yearns and craves for this rest. It is the rest you feel when you wake up early and go out to greet the dawn. A soft breeze is blowing, and you gaze at the rising sun. The soft, orange hues of light work magic inside you, and your heart feels content. Or maybe you feel it sitting beside the ocean, watching seagulls flutter in the wind and gentle waves roll into shore. Your breathing slows, and you sit mesmerized by the combination of wind and waves. Parents often feel it when they hold their children to their chests or watch them as they play with abandon. It is a feeling of wonder that stirs something profound inside.

Everyone I know is familiar with the heart's rest that I have described. Such feelings are part of our internal chemistry and machinery. It is a blueprint of peace that has been placed inside of us by our Creator. Such inner heart rest is the cure for panic, fear, and emotional paralysis. The peace I am talking about has been called "the peace that passes all our understanding."[15] It is a feeling that engulfs the heart and fills it to overflowing. The mind cannot grasp such peace, no matter how hard we try to clutch it. And as much as the mind attempts to contain and define it, it cannot. The glory and brilliance of the sunrise eludes the mind. Only our hearts can feel the wonder and hear the subtle whisperings of this wind.

I suggest you tune into your heart to learn how to listen to this wind, the breeze of love emanating from your heart. I want to share with you how to accomplish your desires. I believe it is *the* most profound method for throwing off the paralyzing anxiety and fear that you have been feeling. It utilizes techniques for quickly and effectively connecting to your own heart. Your heart carries the answers you need to overcome inner anguish and torment. All you need to do is tap into the wisdom, the fountain of love that lives inside of you.

This is called *the Path of Love.* The journey down this path is like no other journey. It is like climbing into a ship that can be called the *Ship of Safety*,[16] a vessel that will carry you across the dark and turbulent waters that cover the face of the earth we live in now. It can transform your world from darkness into a world of light.

As mentioned earlier, anyone can learn the basic techniques of this path. You don't have to change your religion or beliefs using these methods. You can incorporate them into your current spiritual framework. If you don't have a spiritual path, that's all right too. You have a heart. Remember, the Divine Light of the All-Merciful lives inside of you. Your heart, His light, will guide you to where you need to go. It is as inevitable as the sunrise.

The Path of Love has eight essential principles:

1. You must become aware.
2. Reflection on your life is necessary to advance.
3. Return to your heart.
4. You must embrace forgiveness.
5. You must practice gratitude.

The Path of Love

6. You must give yourself hope and mercy.

7. It is essential to utilize *The Remembrance* daily.

8. You need to develop a Daily Heart Connection Practice.

If your heart is troubled and you find these words encouraging, I invite you to continue reading as many other discouraged souls before you have done. Incorporate the principles of *The Path of Love* into your life and find the peace that you so dearly desire.

3

OPEN THE DOOR OF AWARENESS

The ultimate value of life depends upon awareness and the power of contemplation rather than mere survival.
—ARISTOTLE

The door of awareness had been flung open in Gabriel's life. Only one session of deep heart connection had been required to expose a fissure, a crack that was zig-zagging its way through his heart. A revelation of awakening had been exposed like a fault within one of the earth's tectonic plates. Gabriel was being primed for an inner earthquake.

Such a tremendous movement within his heart shouldn't come as a surprise. As I said earlier, our hearts contain the deep inner knowledge of what is needed to create success in our lives. What I am discussing isn't an outer success, not material wealth or achievement. No, I am referring to the success of the heart. It is the knowledge and intelligence that will propel us toward true inner peace and real happiness.

Such wisdom is buried within the mountain of the heart. It is the light that our Creator has infused within us from the time of our birth. The light is a light of love that connects us to mercy and compassion. Indeed, it is our birthright, an inner blueprint for self-healing. All of us have the potential to excavate this intrinsic knowledge and connect to a deep, never-ending river of love.

Gabriel had tapped into this knowledge. During his first healing session, he discovered he had anxiety and fear around developing mental illness. The traumatic experience he had during his time with the young girl in Italy was producing his fear. As a consequence, he was trapped in that prison of a room and forced to relive his inner demons. I had learned from Gabriel's sister that Gabriel had an older sister, Sarah, who also suffered from mental illness that left her locked up in a dark basement room of their house in Rabat, Morocco. She eventually passed away, isolated and forlorn.

Her illness and death had always troubled Gabriel. His experience in Italy only added fuel to his troubled psyche. Similar traumatic events had wormed themselves deeply inside. Horrific movies shrouded his heart, shrouding his inner divine light. Now they were rearing their ugly head, exposing feelings of separation, pain, and panic. They asked him: "Will you end up like your sister, alone and abandoned by your family?"

Such fears created disharmony in his life, resulting in pain, panic, and paralysis. His fear was irrational. He didn't live in Italy or Morocco. He wasn't alone or being abandoned by his family. Unfortunately, the whisperings of his mind wouldn't cease. COVID-19 had unearthed an overpowering, totally illogical crack in his mental armor. The self-doubt of not being the invincible, self-sufficient man who could master any challenge shook the ground beneath his feet.

Gabriel needed to answer the questions: "How can I see this as love? Could I imagine such a horrible experience as being love, allowed by the All-Merciful, the All-Compassionate as a way to guide my life in a new direction? Could it be possible that all these thoughts, these crazy scattered thoughts that are surging through my mind and torturing my body, could be good?"

It seemed unlikely to him. I knew this because I experienced the same feelings nearly thirty years ago. I had struggled to cut my way through a hedge grove of doubt and disillusionment regarding my marriage and my life's purpose. Thankfully, the *Path of Love* had appeared before me, and I had made the same journey I was now asking him to make. Over the years, I have taught hundreds of people to take this same journey. I had high hopes that he would be successful.

One thing was true. For the first time in his life, Gabriel was aware. A door of awareness had been flung open, exposing his deeply unsettled psyche. If you are searching for real peace that will abolish your fears and calm your heart, then know that becoming aware is the first step toward healing. You need to open the door of awareness and take your first step down *The Path of Love*.

A human being whose heart is blind doesn't have awareness. They go through life like a zombie. They scamper to work. They eat. They sleep. They make love, argue, and rush headlong into the outer world. What do I mean by the outer world? The outer world is the world of the self, the world of materialism. The vast majority of people are slaves to the material world. They have surrendered to their desires.

Please understand, it isn't their fault. As young children, we have all been trained to be captivated by materialism. Television, radio, newspapers, the internet, and the constant barrage of Facebook, Instagram, TikTok, and social media have made us creatures of the instant consumer culture. They stoke the fires of desire for material possessions and instant and never-ending stimulation. They push our focus outward. We have been told it's natural and good to want things, to consume without thinking.

The allure of our cell phones, with their never-ending news, fashion, and celebrity infatuation, drives the modern world. The need for instant gratification has an addictive pull that is challenging to overcome.

Indeed, the whole world revolves around consumption and desire. Like monkeys, we have been conditioned to want and need *things*. We want the next shiny new car, the latest dress, the best clothes, the best house. The pull of celebrity status is overwhelming. It is what we are supposed to do. "It's normal," we are constantly told. Thus, we look outwardly for satisfaction. Alcohol commercials tell us that drinking gets us the girl. The subliminal message says, "Drinking will make us happy."

Yet, as we move through life this way, our hearts slowly become clouded. Thicker and thicker veils pull us into the mist. The radiance of the Divine Light embedded within us dims. Our hearts lose their way, masking the awareness of what is essential in life. Veiling of the heart has consequences. Often, we move away from what we know to be correct, truthful, and honest. A hundred-fifty years ago, a person of high moral character was esteemed. Moral strength and character were valued and admired traits. Now, few people talk about the importance of morality and morals. Indeed, if we examine our society, we see that the importance of having good moral values—honesty, integrity, and fidelity—has diminished.

The Path of Love asks us to change how we move through the world and how we view and think of it. The advertising mentality compels us to think only of me, me, me. It's all about the self. What does the self want? What does the self need? What can the self get? A sense of community and connection is absent.

Opening the door to awareness is critical for overcoming the binge of self. Once a person becomes aware, they wake up. They start contemplating their lives and realize they must be headed in the wrong direction. They understand that their life's compass is skewed. It is pointed in a direction that can never lead to true happiness and inner peace. They discover that the outer life can never fulfill them.

We all know this. We buy a car, and it's a great vehicle, so shiny and new. The new car smell is exciting, but in a few months, the newness wears off. It's just a car, a way to get us from place to place. Every material possession is the same. Remember the last time you bought a new dress or new pair of shoes. The excitement of trying them on and imagining how you'd feel when wearing them was intoxicating. But in a few weeks, that feeling evaporated. They are now just a pair of shoes or a dress that you wear. Owning any material possessions is similar—a new watch, the latest cell phone, a widescreen television, or even a house. We can easily become mesmerized by objects, but, quickly, they lose their luster. They morph from captivating, intriguing things we can't live without into plain objects.

This experience teaches us that the material world can never transform our lives, never make us complete and whole. Opening the door of awareness is the first step toward cutting the cord of instant gratification and outer desires. If we awaken our hearts, then the brakes can be tapped. Our headlong rush and preoccupation with the external world can be slackened. We can begin living more from the heart.

I'm not suggesting owning things or having desires is wrong. We need things. We need a place to live, clothing to hide our nakedness, and food to eat. Having a car, a smartphone, or a computer is okay. The desire for a job and a home is good. All I'm suggesting is that we must wake up to the focus of our lives. A Sufi said, "It's important for a person to hold money in their hands but not in their heart."[17] By this, he meant that having money or material possessions is not wrong. Money is useful. It is essential. We need it to pay our electric bill and rent. However, a problem arises when a person's heart becomes so captivated by money that they become unwilling to share. They become a miser, afraid to give to people in need or to those less fortunate. Their sole focus is on money. Money no longer resides in their hand, but it has overtaken their heart.

Awareness demands that we ask, "Where is the focus of my life?" We must begin turning away from the outside and pondering things from an inside perspective: Why is my heart hurting? Why do I feel panic? Why fear?

Gabriel's second session happened on a Saturday morning. It was May, a balmy day in Florida. Outside, the wind was murmuring against the trees. Gabriel had completed his run. He had spent his time by the beach thinking about his life and time in Italy. He still wondered if he would go crazy. The pain had continued, pinching his chest at unpredictable intervals. At night, he continued to lay awake, often racked with panic and fear. *The Remembrance* had helped. It took the edge off, slightly. But, he still questioned, *Why me? Why did this have to happen to me? Why can't I shake the fear and panic?*

I called him on Zoom at about ten in the morning. He answered on the first ring. His voice was tight, somewhat fearful, and agitated. The posture of his shoulders and body suggested an underlying tension. A tight gray athletic shirt made his muscles seem overly prominent. When I looked closely, a subtle, jittery wave flowed across the cloth. His countenance was strained, and the line between his eyebrows was prominently stitched.

"How are things going?" I asked.

"Not that well." A look of concern came over his face. "I'm still not sleeping. I'm still having panic attacks and chest pain."

"It takes time," I said. "Don't worry, you are going to get better. You are going to be well."

"Sometimes I doubt that," he said. "I feel that the pain and fear are going to last forever." His shoulders slumped as he said these words. His gaze shifted downward, and the timbre of his voice trailed off. Clearly, he was depressed.

I reminded him that it had only been going on for eight weeks. Yes, it had been a difficult two months filled with fear, pain, and trips to the doctor. No relief had come from his physicians. "You can't let it paralyze you," I said

"Yes, I know. I've been trying not to let myself be consumed. I went to the doctor a few days ago," he said. "My family physician is finally seeing patients again. She gave me a prescription for sleeping pills. I took one of them, which helped the first night, but they didn't work the next night. She also gave me some medicine for anxiety and depression. I tried it, but I felt drugged. I'm afraid to use the medicine. I'm afraid to get hooked on it. I have a sister who has been on antidepressants for over twenty years. I'm afraid I'll have a real mental illness, an illness that will never go away."

His voice was picking up speed as he talked, like a freight train just starting up, but I knew he would accelerate out of control. "All the memories of my time in Italy have been replaying in my mind," he said.

He launched into a rehashing of that experience. "I remember the steps I had to climb to reach her room. The steps made a horrible noise. It was dark, and the smell inside the room was terrible. Even now, if I go into a public bathroom that smells strongly of urine, I get flashbacks of that awful room. I don't know if I'll ever get rid of those feelings,"

"Let's start moving deeper into your heart," I offered to calm and distract him.

I asked him to get comfortable. Slowly, he moved into a recumbent position. I had him do some deep breathing exercises to relax himself. Once more, I instructed him to place his right hand over where his heart resided and focus on his heart at a deeper level. I suggested he tune into the palpable beating of his heart beneath his sternum. We then started saying *The Remembrance* together.

"Ahhh, Ahhh," he said. The sounds flowed out of his lips and worked down toward the heart. I asked him to repeat *The Remembrance* more deeply so that the tones vibrated his chest. He did this by exhaling into his heart with each word. In a few moments, his breathing began to slow. The look of tension drained from his face.

"Now, I want you to go deeper into your heart today. As we say *The Remembrance*, I want you to visualize walking down a series of steps progressing further into your heart." I softened my voice. "It's a medically proven form of visualization treatment. Let yourself go."

"Okay," he said.

Medical science has proven that guided meditations are an effective way to calm patients.[18] To experience deeper awareness, a client can listen to a recording, generally accompanied by soft music.

"Say Ahhh," I said. He did this. "Now, see yourself walking down into your heart. Visualize steps, and imagine you are descending these steps. Let yourself go down, down, down. Now, say it again, Ahhh," I toned. He repeated his *Remembrance.* We continued doing this for five breaths. I watched as his face softened more and more until the tension in his face had been siphoned away.

"Do you feel relaxed?" I asked.

"Yes," he said. "I feel calm."

"Now keep all your attention on your heart and tell me what you feel."

He was quiet for a few minutes. I continued chanting *The Remembrance*, keeping my heart open and visualizing the energy from my heart, holding him in a cloud of compassion.

"What do you feel?" I asked again.

His voice was soft and distant. "Nothing," he said.

We went back to breathing. Once more, I asked him to imagine walking deeper and deeper into his heart. "See yourself going down further and further," I said. He continued doing *The Remembrance*. We did this for a few more minutes.

"Now, what do you feel in your heart?" I asked.

"I'm starting to feel some tension, a little anxious," he said.

"So, call to your Creator. Ask Him to reveal to you what the tension is about," I said. I watched as he became jumpier. His right hand was restless.

"I'm starting to feel like I do at night. The panic is rising," he said. He started breathing very quickly.

"Return to *The Remembrance*," I said, "Return to the Ahhh."

He did this for a few more moments.

"I see something. I'm at home now. I'm back at our childhood home in Rabat, Morocco," he said. "My older sister, Sarah, is there. She has beautiful long hair down to her waist and large eyes. She's sitting in the salon. The salon is a large room with red couches that wrap completely around the walls. The couches have an Arabic print. Thick Persian rugs are on the floor. I can see the walls. They are bright white and very shiny. Sarah is reading. A book is sitting on her lap. It's a spiritual book, a holy book, I think." I witnessed his facial expression harden. Furrows in his brow popped out.

"Now my father's come into the room," he said. "He's screaming at her. He's calling her an easy woman. He says she's been out seeking men. He says that the neighbors are talking. She's protesting. He's shaking with anger. Now he's taking off his belt, and he's starting to hit her.

"She's screaming, 'No, no. I wasn't seeing anyone. I'm a good girl. I'm a girl of honor.' He's whipping her. I can hear the horrible sound of the belt as it hits her face and chest. My mother comes into the room, She's a very small woman. She's trying to stand between them; now he's hitting Mom.

"'Stop it. Stop it,' she's shrieking, trying to block the belt with her arms. I'm little, eight or ten years old. My father is huge. I feel myself shaking inside. I want to do something, but I'm afraid. He just keeps hitting them."

Gabriel's whole body was trembling at this point. His chest was rigid. His arms were quivering. His breathing fast and furious.

"Go back to your *Remembrance,* go back to the Ahhh," I said.

We said it together, "Ahhh, Ahhh, Ahhh, Ahhh." I asked him to take it deep into his heart. He followed my instructions. Within a few moments, things had calmed. His expression was softer. A tear slid down his face. I watched as he brushed it away.

"Keep your focus, your awareness in your heart. Don't let it move. Now, I want you to ask your heart or your Creator, 'What does this have to do with my anxiety, my pain, and my panic attacks? How are these related'" I said.

I let the words sink into him. I watched his breathing slow. His eyes were closed and his facial expression had a searching quality. I wondered what was happening inside his mind and heart. I softly repeated *The Remembrance,* letting it wash over his being. The Ahhh sound was like music, wafting throughout the room, penetrating and compelling, washing his heart with love. I continued for several minutes. He didn't say anything. He just lay stoically on the couch.

"Are you getting anything?" I asked after a few more minutes.

"Yes," he said. "A feeling has come up into my chest; it's like a light shining on a book. I can read the words written like they are written into my heart."

"What does the writing say? What are the words?" I asked.

"The fear. It's saying that I fear ending up like my sister," he said.

"What do you mean?" I asked.

"My sister developed mental illness. My father was always suspicious that she saw men outside of marriage. She was a beautiful girl with beautiful black hair and laughed a lot. Everyone loved her and was drawn to her, the men especially. In Arabic culture, a woman not having relations outside of marriage is a big thing. People could talk if a girl were seen with a boy outside the house. It could bring dishonor to the family. My father was a very proud man. His reputation was critical to him. He had grown up poor and worked hard to achieve everything he had acquired. The *Cultural Ministry of Morocco* had given him work. Our neighborhood was small. Everyone's ears were always open. My father thought Sarah was seeing someone, a neighbor boy. They went to the same school, and their paths crossed on the bus and in the neighborhood. The neighbors had been talking."

"So, what happened to Sarah?" I asked.

"My father constantly beat her and screamed, accusing her of having relations outside of marriage. His insults and beatings went on for a couple of years. Nosy neighbors were constantly speaking slyly into his ear. One of my aunts, Hya, accused her of the same. Sarah had gone to stay with this aunt for the summer. The aunt's daughters were Sarah's age, but they were homely. No one complimented their appearance, and their school grades were poor. Hafeza was jealous of Sarah's intelligence and beauty. We never knew for sure about what happened during the summer that Sarah stayed with our aunt, but when she returned from my aunt's house, she had begun to be affected mentally. We felt Hafeza's accusations and badgering had traumatized her. Sarah began to change after that summer."

Gabriel paused and wiped his face with his shirt sleeve.

"All of us remembered the day when she came home. We heard her crying in the street. Hafeza was standing next to her, trying to keep her quiet.

"'I'm not loose. I'm not an easy girl,' she shouted at Hafeza. She looked at the neighbors and said it louder. I'm not impure!"

The neighbors stared at my aunt, casting doubting looks and shaking their heads. Hafeza became embarrassed. She grabbed Sarah and pulled her into the house. She made a scandal with my father. She said the neighbors would talk and bring dishonor to the family name.

"She must be an easy girl," my aunt said. "Even she admits it. She was saying it in the street." Sarah began pounding her head on the wall. "I'm not impure. I'm not a bad girl," she said. All of us thought our aunt's jealousy was causing the problems.

Sarah couldn't take the constant accusations. Her honor was a big thing for her. She was a holy girl, praying often and reading her sacred books. Their constant ridicule over that summer drove her mentally over the edge. Something inside her snapped. She started saying strong things, cursing, and seeing people not in the room. We took her to the psychiatrist, and they put her on medicine, but it didn't help.

One day, she just lost it completely. She had a spell. We learned they called it *psychosis*. We took her to the hospital, but we were a poor family. We couldn't afford to have her stay long. The medicine at that time was primitive. My father was embarrassed by her. The neighbors talked, and this further isolated her. My father wouldn't let her go out into the neighborhood any longer. He feared her talking to a boy and having the neighbors gossip. Over time, she became more and more mentally unstable.

My father forced her to stay much of her time in the basement. It was dark and damp, with no windows. Every day when he left for work, he locked her downstairs. A couple of my sisters would care for her, but my father kept her hidden.

"She went downhill quickly. Soon, she became an invalid. She couldn't get up from the bed. My older sisters, Maryam and Hadiya, and my mother cared for her. She lost control of her bowels, and they had to wash and clean her like a baby every day. All of us brothers and sisters couldn't help her. She was alone, so alone. We didn't know what to do. We couldn't disobey our father. One day, I woke up, and my mother said she had died. We didn't know how it happened, but she died in that small, dark basement," he said.

Gabriel finished his story. Sadness overwhelmed him, and he began to cry. Repeatedly, he wiped the tears running down his face.

"So, how does this relate to you?" I asked. "How does it relate to what is happening with your pain and anxiety?"

"It's fear. The fear that I'll end up like my sister, all alone," he said with a gasp.

I asked him to open his eyes and sit up. I nodded my head.

"Some heavy stuff today," I said.

"Yes," he said. "Very heavy."

"I think we are making progress," I said, "What I have experienced with people who do these types of sessions is that when they begin getting revelations about the cause of their anxiety, the symptoms have less of a hold over them. I want you to begin writing in a journal about your feelings and reflections."

"A journal?" he asked.

"Yes, we talked about this earlier, but I'm not sure you are doing it. I'd like you to get a writing journal from a bookstore and begin documenting what happens in our sessions together. Now that you've become more aware, I want you to keep track of your progress."

Although we discussed in our first session about doing daily remembrance, he related that he hadn't acquired the remembrance beads. Once again, I asked him to get a set of prayer beads that contained about one hundred beads. "They can be just a beaded necklace," I said. "I want you to begin doing *The Remembrance* at night just before bed. Find a calm place to do the technique. Turn off the television and your phone. Then, close your eyes. Next, breathe in through your nose, and as you exhale, you'll verbally say, 'Ahhh.' It's like you will be breathing into your heart.

"Tilt your head down as you practice. Try your best to keep your awareness in your heart region, just to the left of your chest bone. You'll say *The Remembrance* using the beads to keep track one hundred times. This way, your mind can relax. You'll move one bead each time you breathe in and out. You'll do one hundred and then pause. Keep your focus on your heart, letting the peaceful feeling seep into your chest. (See the Appendix for more on this.) Begin spending a few minutes reflecting on how you felt during the day. Then you'll want to focus mainly on this memory of your sister. You'll then do a second round of *The Remembrance* and spend 3-5 minutes reflecting again. And I want you to journal what you find out about yourself. Write something about your feelings regarding what happened to your sister. Contemplate how her illness and what happened to her relates to the fear and panic you feel. Begin pondering what is happening in your life. In the beginning, try to spend ten to fifteen minutes every day using this technique."

Gabriel was silent for a moment. He pursed his lips together. "How long will it take before I'm better?" he asked.

"It can happen quickly, often in the first sessions. That's why I say *Inner Peace Now*—because it can be rapid. Other times, it's a process. It may take some time. Some people get better in a day, others in a few weeks, and for others, it can take a few months. God willing, you will get better," I said.

He nodded, but I could tell he wasn't too confident about what I asked him to do. I explained to him that this type of self-examination is a critical skill for troubled hearts.

When life's difficulties darken our lives, we first must embrace awareness. We must ask ourselves, "Where should I shine the light of awareness?" True peace and contentment flourish only when the heart is infused with light. *The Path of Love* suggests that if we want to be healed of the anxiousness that swamps our hearts, we must first become aware. We need to shine the laser of awareness onto the troubles of our lives. We must search ourselves and ask, "Where does my attention lie? Where are my thoughts? What is the focus of my heart and my life?" If we want to go even deeper, we can ask, "How is what is happening to me a blessing?"

Difficulties a blessing? Yes, it's a challenging question, but roadblocks in our lives often prompt us to think outside the box. If we examine our thinking and focus, we can unearth the true direction of our lives. Are we constantly thinking of pursuing women or a husband? Are we obsessed with cars, clothes, or the latest gadgets? Are we worried about social position and status?

As was mentioned earlier, *the key question* is, "Is my life focused on the outside? Am I wholly attached to the material world and my desires?" Too often, the material world is devoid of real love. It's about things. Our inner lives are different. The inner heart values connection love, kindness, and compassion. It longs for peace and tranquility. It craves the peace that lies beyond our understanding of the mind. The outer self cares about something else entirely. Understand that by walking the *Path of Love*, you can come to feel an immense peace that will calm your heart.

A second awareness that can help us on the journey toward inner peace and contentment is that *a power greater than ourselves exists*. Importantly, it is a loving power that gives and nurtures everything in our world. If the idea that all of creation is nurtured stirs up doubt inside you, head out into nature. Watch the majesty of a sunrise. Listen to the babbling of a stream. Feel the wind on your face and tune your ear to the morning songbirds. Take in the uncanny order and precision of it all. Our earth spins in an orbit. Its revolution creates night and day. At night, we sleep and rest our bodies. By day, we perform our duties. Contemplate the fact that every living creature is fed each and every day. Rabbits, birds, insects, snakes, and sharks—most of the creatures in existence don't save or store up food, yet they are continually sustained.

Our bodies are another wonder. Its mysterious, intricate workings point to a higher power. Contemplate something so simple as a cut of our hand. We cut our fingers, and amazingly, the bleeding stops, a scab forms over the cut. Within a few days, the scab falls off, and new skin has replaced the old. Look with the deep eye of the heart, and you will be mesmerized by the workings of the human body. The healing of a cut is a form of love. The All-Loving designed your body to mysteriously heal and care for itself. We don't have to think about it. We don't have to plan it. Our body magically gives and cares for itself. Our food digests by itself. No input on our part is required to hold infections at bay. Innate love and wondrous perfection permeate everything created by the All-Knowing. Yes, pain exists. Suffering occurs, but creatures, not the Creator, create the most.

A third essential awareness is the awareness of the true power of love. For most people, love is an abstract idea, a concept. We can't see love, hold it, or touch it. Of course, we know the feeling of love—the love we feel for our kids, spouses, and parents. But this is about as far as it goes.

My suggestion, and the Sufi Masters' suggestion, is that we consider expanding our ideas about love. Just like electricity, love can do things. Electricity lights our homes. It runs the toaster and the fan and powers our internet connection. Love is also a dynamic force. The Sufis say that when we bring love into our hearts through the practice of *The Remembrance,* it enlivens and electrifies every cell of our bodies. It alters our chemistry and even changes our DNA.

Understand that the All-Loving creates with love. He sustains and nurtures through love. Love is His language, and the power he projects into the world is carried by love. Just like the wind, you can't see it. You can't hold it in your hand. But you can feel it. Think about how love can change your own life. The love you have for, say, your children or your pet? Can't it soften your heart and wash away selfishness? I have clear memories of my father working fourteen hours a day, sleeping just a few hours each night to put himself through medical school to provide for us a better life. This was a genuine experience of love in action.

Remember from Chapter One that I said that the love of the Creator is like a mother's love? Everyone would agree that a mother's love has power. It possesses force. It is real. A mother's love can move mountains. It can build cities. It can bring communities together. Look at the local news. Night after night, they report stories of how love transforms communities. A child dies.

A mother decides that the child will not be forgotten. She rallies the community and engages the politicians, creating a park or a law in the child's name. This is the transformative power of love.

We can go further in understanding the tangible effects of love. The Sufis say that every time you repeat the Name of God as a sacred word, love literally enters the heart. It is as if you turned on a light bulb, and a dark room became visible. If you repeat The All-Loving's Name, the energy of love physically permeates the heart. Engaging in *Remembrance* floods the heart with love, real physical love. This love feeds our hearts. It energizes and enlivens it. It doesn't just remain in our hearts. This love is pumped to all the organs and cells of our body. It nurtures and transforms the cells. Gabriel's story is a witness to the power of *The Remembrance,* the palpable love that pours into the body to change and transform a life.

A fourth awareness we need to understand and validate is that we have not lived up to the potential of the Divine light embedded within our hearts. Like Gabriel, we need the awareness that we have not connected deeply to that light. We have not been peeling away the veils that obscure the heart. This is the *Path of Love*. It is a journey that takes us down the road to unveiling, uncovering the Divine's light and then sharing it.

If we look closely at Gabriel's story, we see it is a true story, a story of truth. I encourage you to see yourself within his trials. Place yourself inside his pain. It's time for you to become aware of your life's direction. Practically, spend ten to fifteen minutes every night utilizing the techniques we will teach later in this book. Get quiet. Connect to your own heart and let it guide you.

Here's what a contemporary Sufi *Guide of the Love* has to say in his introduction to the book *The Book of Love*:

"Love is a journey everyone should consciously and actively take. The journey is more amazing than our greatest aspirations and more miraculous than our most beautiful dreams. The journey leads the wayfarers to personal liberation, whose highlights are love, forgiveness, unconditional compassion, mercy, reconciliation, hope happiness, positive contribution and optimism, with no place at all for repression, original sin, judgment, punishment, guilt, pain, enmity or even death.

This is not just possible; this is real and beautiful. The journey on the path of love is the elixir of an everlasting life of love. There is no shortage of love, just our willingness to embrace it with our whole heart and channel it to others."[19]

Has this been your experience in life? Do you feel love so strongly in your life that it has led to a feeling of liberation and unconditional compassion and mercy? If not, then I hope you now understand the importance of awareness in transforming your life. I also hope you see why I am sharing with you *the Path of Love*. Just a glimpse of this love, a brief peek as it moves into your heart, is often enough to sustain a person. Practicing *the Remembrance* can give you that glimpse.

As you continue reading, take time to examine and reflect. The panic and fear you feel may seem overwhelming, but it doesn't have to control your life. You can become well. Your heart can be healed. Practice the exercises I give you and continue your journey. You won't be disappointed.

4

REFLECT UPON YOUR LIFE

Without reflection, we go blindly on our way.
—MARGARET J. WHEATLY

Gabriel's work for the next session was to contemplate and reflect. In just a couple of sessions he had pulled back the curtains of traumatizing emotional issues buried deep within his heart. Hidden traumas shouldn't remain hidden. Numerous medical studies have shown that traumas have long-ranging effects on a person's health. They can create anxiety and depression and lead to substance abuse and self-harm. In addition, they can create heart disease.[20]

Concealed trauma controls how we respond to other people and events in our lives in subtle ways. It determines our motivations and, often, our choices in life. If we don't deal with the emotional scars, peel back the scabs, and let the flow of love heal our wounds, then we may find ourselves moving through life wounded, unable to experience and give love in the way that would serve our highest good.

Gabriel had been a victim in a family of abuse. He had repressed his hurts and emotional injury, but these feelings still lived inside him. The events still had a powerful hold on him. The layers and layers of injury had crystalized within his heart and hardened. COVID-19 struck him like a lightning bolt, cracking the emotional armor he had built around his heart and exposing the inner tectonic fault. Our healing sessions had laid bare the raw experiences of inner torment that lay within him. Such exposure wasn't bad. Unearthing the crack was a positive event. It would lead to his ability to heal.

As I said earlier, within difficulty and pain lies the loving plan of the All-Merciful. Without the "tragedy" of such a life storm, Gabriel wouldn't have been experiencing panic attacks. He wouldn't have agreed to healing sessions. His perception was that life had been good before the upheaval. In his mind, his heart was fine. It was normal. In his early thirties, he was busy working, trying to make money. He was pursuing women, hitting the bars, and chasing what he planned for his life—all the usual things a man his age might do.

He wasn't focused on moving deeper into his heart. He wasn't planning on reflecting upon himself. His focus was outward. But the All-Compassionate had other plans. Whenever our life falls far from its proper direction, the most loving sends a message, a call of love, to redirect us. Sometimes, the call is transmitted gently, the voice of a book nudging us. Speech carried like a spring breeze. Other times, it is deafening, a trumpet blast of strength and power in the form of an emotional hurricane. The All-Merciful calls us to reexamine the direction of our lives.

The pain and inner anguish that Gabriel felt was such a call. This had upended Gabriel's life. Now he had a choice: look deep, question and reflect on his life's direction, or ignore the warning.

In *Dark Nights of the Soul,* former monk Thomas Moore suggests that if we ignore a violent emotional life storm by burying our head in the sand, we may remain stuck.[21] Such events meant to propel us emotionally and psychologically may remain. The pain we feel over a lost spouse or another loss may not slacken. It may continue to toss us on the waves of the storm. We shouldn't be afraid of such times of trial. Rather than seeking avoidance, we need to practice our dance steps. We must focus on sliding, twirling, and twisting, deftly navigating the storm.

Outward events can also call us. Do you think COVID-19 will be the only tiny virus headed our way? Rumors of newer, even more horrific viruses have surfaced in the news. SARS, Ebola—what will COVID-19 eventually become?

Are these horrible events just chance? They might be, but the truth is inescapable. Our lives are being upended, people are suffering. Our hearts need healing.

Gabriel's next session happened the following week.

"Hi, Gabriel," I said to him on Zoom. "How have you been feeling since we last met?" He looked reasonably good over the internet. Calmness spanned his face. It was morning, and light from his balcony gave him a soft glow.

"I'm doing a little better, he said. The pain is less. I'm still having panic attacks. They are still coming fairly regularly. I'm doing *The Remembrance.* It helps but hasn't gotten rid of the panic attacks."

"How does that make you feel?" I asked.

"I feel stuck, stuck in a place that I don't want to be," he said. He adjusted himself in his seat. His frustration was visible.

"Yes, it's normal to want to be rid of a problem," I said.

I relayed to him the story of a woman whose life had been sidetracked by crippling anxiety and years of panic attacks. But the session had brought up anxiety and pain. She abandoned the work after two sessions.

"But you are not like that," I said. "You've got real courage. You're willing to do the deep work. You've had only two sessions; this is our third. It's been over a month since we started working together. That's a very short time. You are actually moving very quickly. In just two short sessions, you've identified some of the causes of the pain and panic. This is good. It means your heart is open to change. It would be best if you patted yourself on the back. Most people would be scared to do this type of work. They would be unnerved if they had to examine the past traumas of their lives. They would rather push them deep inside."

I watched as he shifted himself on the couch.

"Sometimes I want to do that," he said. "I want just to go back to the life I had before this disaster and forget about all the troubles of my life."

I nodded. Of course, this is the usual way most people approach life. They bury their heads in the sand when faced with severe emotional trauma. Unfortunately, the wounds don't disappear. Deep inside, they still grip the heart, creating pain and inner sadness.

"Do you think I'll ever be well?" he asked.

"Yes, I do," I said. "Remember, I've worked with hundreds of people like you, and nearly all of them have gotten well. I want you to have hope. You can be better. I am certain you can return your life to where it was before. The question is, do you want to return to life as it was before you became ill?"

Gabriel twisted his lips to the left, thinking. His words came out in a measured cadence. "My life was pretty good before. I had a job, money, and was looking for a wife."

"Was your life headed in a good direction?" I asked.

"I had a plan for my life," he said. "I would work for five more years and save enough money to buy a car and a house. Now it's all in limbo. The economy is in the dumps. I've lost my job and have no idea when I'll get it back like before."

"Yes, the best-laid plans of mice and men," I said, "often go awry. Why do you think that is?" I asked. "What do you think the Creator is planning for you? What did you get when you did your reflections this past week?"

He shrugged his shoulders, glancing downward. The light flickered back and forth across his face like shadows dancing. "I don't know. I didn't get anything. I did *The Remembrance* as you asked me. I did one hundred and then focused on my heart. I listened, but nothing came to me. I didn't get any feelings or answers."

His shoulders slumped even further. He broke direct eye contact.

"Not to worry," I said. "You will. The more you connect to your heart, the more answers will come. Keep connecting. Keep doing *The Remembrance* and focusing your attention and intention inside your heart region."

"What do you mean by that? Focus and intention?" he asked.

"Whatever a person focuses on is magnified. Focusing on

your heart makes your emotional images and pictures easier to see. Focus is like looking into a room and shining a light to find something," I explained. "If I ask you right now how your left elbow feels, your mind will immediately make you aware of your elbow. Before I said this, your attention was somewhere else. Perhaps you were thinking about what you were going to eat for dinner. You were not aware of how your elbow was feeling. Now that you have decided—set an intention—to become aware of your elbow, all of your consciousness has moved to that location. Now you are aware of what your elbow feels like. Perhaps recently you strained your elbow, and it was mildly sore. When you focused on making dinner, your elbow soreness escaped your consciousness. Once you shine the light of your focus onto your elbow, you suddenly become aware of the feelings of your elbow.

"The intention is about deciding to do something. It is making a choice. When you do *The Remembrance,* you are choosing to examine your inner heart. When you do this, your consciousness and focus must be in the heart region, just to the left of your breastbone. Your heart is here," I said, tapping my chest with my hand. "You want to place your focus on the area three inches below the skin. Your awareness and consciousness will move to this area when you do this. As you breathe out and say Ahhh, imagine your breath going into the place where you have shone the light of your focus. Doing this will keep your focus in your heart region."

"Okay," he said.

"It will come. Just give it time," I said.

He replied with a nod. He didn't seem sure of things. I understood that it was hard in the beginning to have hope. When a person still feels pain and panic and is totally disconnected, it's challenging to see the light at the end of the tunnel.

"I would like to know more about your father and the circumstances of your life growing up in Morocco," I said.

He stopped his fidgeting on the couch. Pausing to think, his right hand came up to his face, and he stroked his jawline.

"We were poor, very poor. We lived in the capital city of Morocco, Rabat," he said. "It is a city of a couple of million people. People live tightly packed in the neighborhood. They are piled upon each other in narrow winding streets made of red bricks."

I let him continue with the story, probing deeper into the events that had shaped his life.

"My first memory was of a tiny apartment," he said. "My father had rented a small four-room place in a dirty neighborhood a few miles from the city center. It was one level, with a concrete floor. The walls were also made of hard concrete and painted bright, shiny white. All six sisters, two brothers, and my father and mother were squeezed inside. I remember the place only had two lights and single bulbs hanging from the ceiling. One was in the living room, which we called the salon, and the other was in the kitchen. I wouldn't even call the kitchen a room. It was more like a closet, four feet wide and deep. In those days, we didn't have a real stove. A portable propane grill like the one you take camping was all we had. We used candles in the other rooms."

He laughed and said, "I remember one time Sarah had been reading her schoolwork at night just before bed. She had situated the candle in the middle of the book. She fell asleep without putting out the candle. The book had this big burn hole right in the middle of it. It had burned to the back of the book. When she picked up the book, it fell apart like a dead chicken." He laughed again. "Of course, she couldn't tell my father—that would have been a real beating."

"We didn't even have running water. This was nineteen seventy-five. A community faucet was located about fifty yards from the house. The girls would take these big plastic milk jugs and trek down to the faucet every day. They would fill them with water. Every room had a large, brown clay urn in the corner with a ladle. The toilet was just a hole in the floor that went to the city plumbing system. A water urn was in there as well. Every time you went to relieve yourself, you had to flush the toilet paper down the hole.

"The amazing thing was how Sarah could make the place shine. She white-washed the walls every few months, draped Arabic carpets on the walls, and kept the place spotless—mopping the floors and sweeping every day. She had a way of folding the blankets and sheets to make it incredibly organized, like someone staging a house for sale. We didn't have much, but we were happy. At least we were happy when my father wasn't around.

"The kids all shared the same room. We had no mattress, just blankets piled on the concrete floor. We slept together, bunched together like a litter of newly born puppies. Every day after school, if we weren't outside playing, we'd all be together and crammed into the salon. We laughed. we sang, and we danced. An old Motorola radio, brown, with this scratched dial placed on a small plastic table, was pushed into one of the corners. My sisters would always listen to *Madonna, Sting*, or some other Western singer—and they'd be singing along in high voices, gyrating about the room. My brother David and I danced with them. David was small. They'd swing him around and around until he was dizzy. Everything would be great until my father got home.

"My father didn't arrive home from work until six. He got off earlier, but we didn't have a car. We didn't have the money for one of the small blue taxis that roamed the city. In those days, they were cheap, only twenty cents, to get you from the city center, but we couldn't afford even the blue taxi. So my father walked home. It was four or five miles from his job with the Cultural Ministry downtown.

"So, we'd all be laughing and playing. Suddenly, we'd hear it *bam, bam, bam*, my father would hammer on our front door. The door was solid oak, the only nice thing about the apartment. It was stained a rich black color and had hand-engraved markings. The landlord said it had been imported from Spain. He had confiscated it from an old government building in the city.

"The pounding on the door identified my father's arrival at home. I'll never forget that sound. The oak door boomed like a war drum, reverberating throughout the tiny apartment. It was a ferocious sound of instilling tremendous angst. My father couldn't knock like a normal person. No, it was like a king being announced. We knew he was saying, 'The king is home.'

"Instantly, the music was quelled. The dancing evaporated, and fear filled the room.

"'Your father is home,' my mother would screech. 'Line up. Line up.'"

"She'd scamper to the door and all of us kids would race to form a line from the oldest to the youngest. My father advanced into the room and took a seat on the sofa. Sitting regally, he would hold out his hand palm down. All of us kids would have to come forward, bend down with strained smiles, kiss his hand, and say, 'Welcome home, father.' It was a ritual he demanded every night.

"Generally, a scowl was all we got in return. And then the terror would begin. Once, I remember my mother cooking the food we had for dinner. The 'King' marched into the salon. We had prepared the room just for him. All the blankets we slept on were stacked against the wall, and a small, rickety wooden table was placed in the center. A heaping portion of couscous, some vegetables, and a small piece of chicken was gingerly placed in front of him.

"We all crowded nervously around after he had sat down. My father always ate first, and, of course, he ate the meat. After he finished, we kids would eat the leftovers. If there weren't much to eat that day, my mother wouldn't eat.

"'Is this all you have?' he screamed one day. He had taken one bite and then slammed the plate at her feet. He pulled her down by the hem of her dress and slapped her. 'You're the worst cook in the neighborhood.' He'd grabbed her by the neck and forced her down on her hands and knees to clean up the food he'd knocked to the ground.

"I cowered in the corner, trying to be as small as possible. He glowered at us, demanding to know our latest grades. We all knew that if our answer weren't to his satisfaction, he'd rip his leather belt from around his pants and proceed with a beating."

Reflect Upon Your Life

Gabriel began trembling. The images from his childhood hung in the air like a black, impenetrable fog.

I could tell it was time to proceed

"Okay, let's start going deeper into your heart," I said.

Unlike traditional counseling, the Sufi healing sessions don't consist of just talking. We often begin with a general conversation to put the client at ease, recapping our previous efforts. We explore new psychological or emotional issues that have arisen in response to the earlier work. After this five-minute introduction, we focus deeply on the client's heart. We utilize a unique combination of sound and breath to create an emotional opening. A sacred sound for the Divine is chanted. It can be the syllable Ahhhh, the universal sound people make when they feel relaxed. Sometimes, people prefer an actual name for God. Often, they wish to utilize the Aramaic word for God, *Allahu*. Other people like using Jehovah and accenting the Ahhh syllable. Still others are comfortable saying Allah.

The person slows their breathing. Utilizing vibrational sound and breath in this fashion frequently moves them into a slightly altered state of consciousness or deep relaxation. Here, the pictures and images of the unconscious heart can come forward.

A person can stop at any time if they feel uncomfortable or anxious.

I asked Gabriel to get well situated, and once again, we began with breathing exercises for a deeper state of relaxation. This took a few minutes. Soon, his posture suggested that he was relaxed.

"Okay, now let's start *The Remembrance*," I said. "Breathe in deeply, and with each breath you breathe out, just say, Ahhh.

Let the sound flow down into the heart. Feel it like a wave of relaxation."

Gabriel followed my directions. The energy and flow of the Divine Remembrance washed over his heart, taking him deeper and deeper. I watched as his body calmed. His arms went loose at his sides, and the air in the room became less dense.

"Now, what do you feel in your heart?" I asked.

"I don't feel anything," he said.

I studied him closely. His face was placid. His arms and legs hung limply at his sides.

"Let yourself go deeper. Move back to *The Remembrance*," I said. Over and over, he toned his sacred word for God. Each time he exhaled, the sound moved into his chest.

"I'm feeling something now," he said. "I see something. It's nighttime. I'm lying in bed. It feels like a week or so ago when I had a horrible panic attack. I can see my body getting tighter and tighter from the pain."

As he said these words, his body began reflecting the vision of what he saw inside his heart. His wrists shook, and his upper chest became tense.

"What are you feeling now?" I asked

He was completely stiff.

"I'm stuck," he said. "It's like a paralysis. I can't move. It's dark, so dark, and I can't move. I'm paralyzed, completely paralyzed."

Gabriel's breathing became harsh, with a deep guttural quality.

"Come back to *The Remembrance*," I said. "Come back to Ahhh."

We did this together. It was slow. His body looked like a

corpse, stiff and lifeless. He appeared incapacitated. His voice came out in short, choked spasms.

I said the words for him.

"Take my voice into your heart; take it deep," I said. He lay there listening, quivering.

"I can't move. I can't breathe. The pain's awful—so sharp, so strong," he said loudly. "I feel just like I do when I'm having a panic attack. It's the same."

He moaned softly; a few tears welled up in his eyes.

"Let yourself relax. Take the sound inside. Let it move deeper and deeper into your heart."

We did *The Remembrance* together, longer this time. It was as if the sound was pouring light into his chest.

"Now I want you to ask your heart," I said, "'What is this paralysis about? Why can't I move?'"

Silence stifled the room. I carried on with *The Remembrance* and waited for him. As I watched his face, I could see his mind working. I could sense that an answer was coming to his heart.

"The paralysis is fear. I'm afraid," he said.

"What else do you see?" I asked.

"I'm back in Morocco again. I'm standing there, and my father has his belt out, and he's screaming at me. I'm four or five years old. I can't do anything. I'm powerless. Now he's beating me," he said.

Rigidity strained Gabriel's body further. Now his breath was shallow and rapid. A mask of panic and fear contorted his facial muscles. The look was wild and sad—like the picture of fear and doom of a cornered animal who knows he is soon to be slaughtered. Saliva seeped from the right side of his mouth.

"I want to run. I want to escape, but I can't move. I'm frozen," he said.

"Return to *The Remembrance*," I said. "Say the words." I continued saying Ahhh, Ahhh, Ahhh, but louder. I directed the words and aimed them at his heart. Slowly, he began to follow, but his voice was soft and far away. I urged him to say them louder. "Take them into your heart." Soon, he returned to saying *The Remembrance,* taking the light into his chest.

Once his mood had calmed, I asked him to call his Creator or his heart to ask what the message was, the teaching for him about the paralysis. To ask, "What is the All-Merciful trying to show me?" Gabriel was silent as he connected to his heart. I waited patiently. It took one or two minutes.

"I'm getting something," he said. "I'm seeing my life as it was before the panic and pain. I was strong. I was a real man. Nothing could stop me. I believed in myself. I was following the plan for my life that I had envisioned."

"How does this relate to your panic attacks now?" I asked. "What is the connection?"

He was silent again. A look of contemplation and thinking graced his face.

"I'm disabled with fear and hopelessness. It's like when I was a child, and I couldn't do anything about my father. I was helpless. I'm afraid that I'll be helpless. I won't be a man anymore."

"Go back to why the All-Loving is showing you this. What is he trying to teach you?" I asked.

Once again, he was silent. We returned to the opener, *The*

Remembrance of the Divine Light. Over and over, we said the words together, letting them work their magic of opening. It only took a short time.

"I'm getting something again," he said. "It's like a message swirling within a mist."

"What does it tell you?" I asked.

"It's like I believed in *my* power, *my* strength. The message is that I believed and placed my trust in things on the outside. I was caught up in the outside world, the shiny things, the material things of life. I wasn't looking within," he said.

"Why is this happening to you? What does the All-Loving want you to do?" I asked.

Silence enshrouded the room. Gabriel's face was blank. We went back to *The Remembrance*, toning it melodiously.

"Stay with your heart," I said as I felt him drift away, afraid. "Look within."

More silence. His body was again immobile. I waited and waited some more.

"What do you feel?" I asked again. "What is the message? What should you be doing?"

"I don't feel anything," he said. "I don't get any messages. I don't know."

I waited a few more minutes then asked him to sit up.

I encouraged him not to judge himself because he couldn't see the complete answers. This was normal. A deep opening could take some time. I explained that his homework was to continue his contemplation at night. He was to get calm and do *The Remembrance* for fifteen to thirty minutes. Next, he was to focus on his heart and ask his Creator what he should do with his life. He was to also keep writing in his journal, to write down anything that came to him. We agreed to meet the following week.

What does it mean to reflect?

Reflection means sitting quietly, spending time in the stillness, and pondering. I recommend that you reflect in the night, one to three hours before dawn, because the night is a time of calmness.[22] The world's noise has shrunk—pulled back into itself. Distractions are at a minimum. Our bodies are also subdued. The sympathetic nervous system, the adrenaline-driven hormone state that stimulates us, has been curbed. Now, the parasympathetic sleep-inducing hormonal system has begun to predominate. Our subconscious mind is aroused, and emotional insight is heightened. The Sufis, the great lovers of the Divine, encourage people to "take advantage of the night."[23] At night when the chatter of the day has calmed, the world sleeps, and the connection to the Divine is more easily obtained. They say that this is the time that the All-Compassionate, All-Loving is most near.

What should you be reflecting on?

Ask yourself: Could the trouble and tribulations and all the difficulty of my life be a message? Could it be a teaching for me? In this time of contemplation, you should focus on your heart, the place just to the left of your breastbone. As you ask these questions, listen to your heart for the answers.

Next, you can move deeper. You can ask: Could all the turmoil and calamity that has besieged my life possibly be love? A loving hand reaching out to me to direct me? Of course, this may seem quite impossible to you. Love wrapped inside a disaster? Love moving through tragedy? But if you are willing to take a leap of faith to broaden your thinking and dispel your doubts, ask these questions of your heart or your Creator.

What does that loving hand want from me?

Not from me but for me?

Let's recap: We started this journey by becoming aware. Awareness is the door. A person cannot move deeper into the heart without first going through the door of awareness. We have to know that something is wrong with our life. We have to wake up. Life storms—divorce, illness, loss of someone we hold dear—could be a stimulus for this awareness. Not only for Gabriel but for everyone in the world. Reflection is putting one foot forward to the next step. It is the start down the path of seeing with the inner eye of the heart.

Real reflection means connection. It means that we begin the process of connecting deeply to our hearts. We need to connect to the inner light, the Divine light that pulsates within our hearts. If we sit down each evening and become still, our hearts can begin to speak. It is essential to shut out the noise of the outer world. Turn off the radio and television. Put aside our cell phones. Begin reflecting upon our lives by first placing our focus and consciousness centered within our hearts. Set the intention to be open to the Divine Light.

Connection to that light will give us the knowledge and wisdom we need to succeed in life. As I said earlier, this isn't outer success. It is the real success of the heart—the opening to a continual outpouring of love. Success in the outer life means things and more things: cars, clothes, houses. The success we are seeking lives in the heart.

Please begin spending fifteen to twenty minutes each night in contemplation and reflection. Let the messages of your heart come forward. If we ask the All-Loving, He will respond.

At the end of this book, I have made available audio and video downloads that you can listen to and watch that will guide you in this reflection process.

Take a chance, and reflect upon your life.

5

RETURN TO YOUR HEART

Love is what we are born with.
Fear is what we learn.
—MARIANNE WILLIAMSON

Gabriel came online for the next session a few weeks later. We opened with some general conversation. I wanted to get a sense of how he had been doing since our last meeting. Throughout the past couple of months, he had slowly been making progress. The severe emotional fits of panic, pain, and sleeplessness had lessened. The storm shaking his life was still swirling, but he had started to get his footing.

His mental outlook had improved, even though he still had concerns about the speed of his recovery. The pain still coursed through his chest in fits and starts. He had left Florida for ten days and gone to Washington, D.C., to visit his sister, Ava. He thought that being out of his usual location would help.

Gabriel said the trip had started fine, but then they had car trouble. They had gone over a bump in the road about fifty miles from their sister's house, and something had happened to the car's axle. They had to have the car towed to a repair shop. His sister's husband, Jake, had to take off work to drive down and get them. Jake was angry and couldn't hide it. He made Gabriel feel unwelcome. It was going to be nine hundred dollars to have the axle repaired. His unemployment checks had started, so he was okay financially, but the situation with his brother-in-law had been emotionally troubling.

For the first two days in Washington, he felt fine. His sleep had improved. Soon, however, his family started discussing COVID-19, and then he found out that Jake was also having emotional issues. He, too, suffered from depression. On the third night in their house, Jake had a panic attack. Feeling the husband's fear and anxiety caused Gabriel's issues to heighten. He and his brother stayed ten days in Virginia and then came home.

Today, as we started his session, he looked exhausted and down. Dark eyes and a drained expression choked his face. He was doing *The Remembrance* often but was only sleeping a few hours each night. As we continued our conversation, it was my impression that even though he seemed down emotionally, he wasn't experiencing actual clinical depression. His appetite was good. He found enjoyment in running and being out in nature. Also, his mood varied. He didn't always feel troubled. Often, he even felt hopeful. I'm not a clinical psychologist or psychiatrist. It's important for people who experience these symptoms to check with their physician.

Gabriel's dark emotions seemed tied to his travels to his sister.

"For the last three days, I have been on my own, silent," he said. "I don't talk; I'm not myself. I've always been a happy, outgoing guy, talkative and fun. Now, I'm changing; being worried about this illness is changing me. I don't even like being around people that much."

As he spoke, I watched his body language. I could sense he was still afraid that he would never be well. He looked rattled. He spoke haltingly, and he gazed off to the left. I asked him if my impression was correct.

"Yes, it's true," he said. "I'm afraid life will never be back the way it was before."

Gabriel's feelings are common among people who are suffering from an illness. Many of my patients have a similar dread. Such fear and doubt are unsettling. We all have our comfort zones—beliefs and attitudes about how life should be. When our lives don't cooperate, and we get pummeled by the storms of life, it's natural to feel out of sorts. Anxiety and depression are common.

With his last words, Gabriel's head dropped further forward. He slumped down on his couch. Fatigue and worry creased his face.

"What do you do to feel better?" I asked.

"When I do *The Remembrance,* I feel better," he said. "My heart is lighter, and the anxiety and fear pass. When I'm feeling bad, my negative thoughts deaden me. The black ideas take over my brain, and I can't shake them."

I nodded.

"I feel like my whole brain is swollen, and I'm going to explode. His hands reached up to cradle his skull. I fear I'm losing myself. It's like I don't know who I am anymore," he said.

"But *The Remembrance* helps, right?" I asked.

"Yes, when I make the time to sit quietly early in the morning or just before bed, and I do *The Remembrance,* my heart feels light," he said, pausing. "The black ideas are pushed into the background. They don't consume me any longer, and I feel at peace. When I reach that state, I feel all I want is peace. I want to feel and know the peace."

"Humm," I said, listening to him and watching him closely. I could tell his heart was ready. A couple of months of *The Remembrance* had been working inside of him. He was indeed changing, traveling deeper into his own heart.

"Let's start moving deeper into your heart," I said. "Why don't you get comfortable." I watched as he moved back on the couch. He lay partially reclining, with his head tilted backward.

"Let's start with the relaxation breaths," I said.

Once again, I guided him through deep breathing exercises designed to calm and relax him. We did this for three or four minutes. Watching his posture, I saw his muscles loosen and some of the tension leave him.

"How are you feeling now?" I asked.

"Relaxed," he said.

"Okay, let's do *The Remembrance* together," I said.

We began using his sacred word for God, again taking the "Ahhh" sound deep into the heart region. We continued for about two minutes.

"Now, how does your heart feel?" I asked.

"Calmer, much calmer," he said.

"I would like you to let your consciousness move deeper into your heart and ask your Creator why this has happened to you,"

I said. 'Why the panic, fear, and paralysis?' Ask, 'What is the lesson I am supposed to learn?'"

Over the last month, I had been encouraging him to reflect on his life. The key issue for him was *Why Me? Why Now?* This question was an important clue to help him understand how the All-Loving was silently guiding him through the disaster that had befallen him.

We moved back to *The Remembrance*, the Ahhh, Ahhh, Ahhh, taking it deeper and deeper into the heart. I felt he was all up in his head, with dark ideas swirling around. I could see it as his body posture and facial expression had changed. When we tried to move deeply, his body became rigid.

"Are you getting any answers?" I asked.

"No, nothing," he said.

Once again, we returned to *The Remembrance*. I asked him to say it with me. Together, we sent the energy of love down, down, down into his heart, using the words like a hypnotic musical potion to vibrate his heart. I sensed that we needed to continue this for a more extended period. We let *The Remembrance* work its magic on Gabriel's heart for five whole minutes. Slowly, I began to see movement across his face. It was like he was traveling.

"Now, what can you feel?" I asked.

"I see myself. I'm back in Morocco. I'm fourteen or fifteen. It's early evening. It's a sunny, beautiful day. Not too hot. A light wind is blowing the grass. I'm playing soccer with my friends in a small vacant lot near our house. We played for hours and hours until it was too dark to play.

"Now I'm walking through the front door of our home, and my father is waiting for me. He is angry.

"'Where have you been?' he's saying. His voice is high and tight.

"'Playing soccer with my friends,' I said, unsure why he was so angry.

"He grabs me by my ear and pulls me through the house.

"'You were supposed to be back here working, helping to paint the basement with your brothers,' he says. Now, he's shoving me against a wall. He has his fingers around my throat. He's choking me."

Gabriel was shaking. The fear of the memory had overtaken his body.

"Go back to your heart," I said. "Go back to *The Remembrance*." I began saying the Ahhh, Ahhh, Ahhh. Slowly, he began to join in. His voice was jerking.

"I can feel the anxiety starting in my chest," he said.

"What do you feel," I asked, "in your heart?"

"I feel sad, worthless, and angry. Mostly angry," he said.

"Angry?" I asked.

"Yes, angry at my father for how he treated me and my sisters. Angry about how he beat us and my mother. Angry that this calamity has messed up my life," he said.

I watched as he slumped down further into the couch. His expression was of despair.

"Let's go back," I said. I began toning Ahhh, Ahhh, Ahhh.

He returned his concentration to his heart, placing his feelings and awareness near his left sixth rib. I asked him to let his breath penetrate further. We continued again for a long period, letting the sounds wash and lift his heart. Soon, I could see a change in his facial muscles.

"Now, I'd like you to repeat the question from earlier," I said. "Ask your Creator, Why has this been happening to me? What is the deeper message that the All-Merciful is sending to me?"

Silently, he asked those questions.

We went back to *The Remembrance* to open the heart.

"Are you getting anything?" I asked him after a few minutes.

"Yes, I see that I needed to move away from my old way of life. The bar-hopping, partying, and chasing women. I need to get rid of the anger I feel. It has caused problems in my job and with the girls I was dating," he said. "I see now that the focus of my life was wrong." He paused. "I wasn't thinking about anything but the outside world."

I let this awareness sink in. Gabriel was silent for a full two minutes, letting *The Remembrance* work in his heart.

"How do you feel now?" I eventually asked.

"Much better. The sadness and panic are gone," he said. "Now I feel real peace."

I asked him to open his eyes and sit up.

I said, "I know that you are frustrated with the difficulties that have upended your life, frustrated with the continual problems with your fear, anxiety, and insomnia. But we are making progress. You are getting messages and answers to the questions you are asking about your life."

"But the paralysis," he said. "I'm tired, so tired of feeling stuck in my life. I can't seem to shake all these dark thoughts. They just keep coming."

"Yes, that too. But do you see how this has been necessary?" I asked. "Can you see that without this extreme difficulty, you would not have been motivated to change your life?"

He looked thoughtful for a second. "Yes, I can see that in my mind."

Your brother tells me that your anger has improved.

"Yes, I used to be angry all the time. I never knew why. I would lash out at people often for no reason. And I never knew what to do about it. I tried to ignore it. I would go out and have fun, never really looking at what was making me angry," he said.

"What is the wisdom?" I asked. "This is what you need to focus on in your contemplation time. This disaster has put you into such an anxious state that it has made you look at your life, reflect, and look for the cause."

"Maybe it relieved me from my past. I had too many issues. I used to ignore them and not go there. By having this anxiety, I have learned that it's time to face my fear," he said.

"This is your work for the next few weeks, to contemplate how this difficulty has been a lesson in your life," I said. "Try to go deep with it. Let yourself connect more fully with your heart."

He nodded. "I'll try my best."

As we ended the session, I agreed inwardly. It was working. He was beginning to return to his heart.

What does it mean to *Return to Your Heart*? As we have suggested earlier, we often think that our brain is what makes us a person. Frequently, we believe that our thoughts control us. Indeed, we are thinking creatures, and how we think can profoundly influence our mental framework and our outlook on life. We can think positively or negatively. Thoughts are infused with power. We can't ignore their contribution to the healing process.

Return to Your Heart

I would suggest that the true source of what makes us human is not our brain. It is our hearts.

We have shown earlier work from the HeartMath Institute demonstrating that tens of thousands of neurons exist within the chest cavity. They surround and penetrate our physical hearts. Scientifically, it has been shown that our heart influences and may even control portions of our brain. The emotions we feel may not originate from the mind.[24]

Think about the last time you felt love for your wife, child, or perhaps your pet. Pause for a moment and go back to that feeling. Where in your body did you feel this sensation? Was it in your head? Or in your breast region? For most people, warm feelings of love are not felt in the head or mind. For almost everyone, the feeling of love is felt in the chest region. The experience happens inside our hearts. I call this area the *emotional heart*. It is the place of feelings and intuition.

Our culture and language show us the importance of our emotional heart. Examine these idioms: "He's got heart," "Let's get to the heart of the matter," or "Don't lose heart." Our language incorporates many other similar expressions. When a person goes to make a vital decision about the direction of their life, they "search their heart." Of course, they have thoughts and weigh ideas, but the final decision often comes down to a heart-guided feeling. True wisdom lives inside our hearts. It is a wisdom that defies logical explanation.

In his book *Love, Medicine, and Miracles,* cancer surgeon Dr. Bernie Siegel shares many stories of patients whose lives were transformed when they began to experience "knowings" about an undiagnosed cancer hidden in their bodies.[25] It was like their body began speaking to them. This intuitive knowledge was often felt within the heart region within their chests.

Our hearts also possess their own memory, apart from the memory we attribute to our brains. Heart transplant recipients give us evidence of this separate "heart memory." In the book *The Heart's Code*, Paul Pearsall, Ph.D., relates how numerous people's habits, likes, and dislikes changed after they received someone else's heart.[26] One compelling story focuses on an eight-year-old girl who began having scary memories post-heart transplant. The donor of her heart had been murdered, and no assailant had been apprehended. Not long after she received her new heart, she began having recurring memories of the assault. She was able to provide evidence of who had killed her donor. Such stories help corroborate our understanding of our heart's separate memory and its intuitive knowledge.

After Gabriel's session, I had the opportunity to talk with another one of his sisters, Sanaa. I wanted to better understand Gabriel's past. His sense of abandonment was strong, aggravating his feelings of isolation. I called his sister Sanaa on the phone.

"Gabriel was a sickly child," she said. "When he was six months old, a severe stomach illness overtook him, He vomited constantly. He lost so much weight that we all began to worry about him. My mother, Hadiya, was breastfeeding, and every time she fed him, he would spit up the milk. My Aunt Hafeza, who was college-educated, tall, and sophisticated, suggested she stop breastfeeding and give him lentil soup with meat. It didn't help. The vomiting continued, and he just got thinner and thinner.

"Finally, after multiple visits to the local general practitioner, Hafeza recommended that we take him to a pediatric specialist. Gabriel, Hafeza, myself, and my mother went to the doctor's office. The physician had been trained in Paris at a famous University. His office was in a prestigious area of Rabat, Morocco. The office was furnished expensively. Modern furniture and valuable-looking glass vases adorned the room. The physician's exquisite framed medical school diplomas and credentials hung on the walls. My mother was from the country, very poor, and uneducated. She couldn't read or write. All the other patients waiting in the office were dressed elegantly in Western clothes. They were wealthy and very light-skinned from never being exposed to the sun. They all stared at my mother, who was dark, wearing a faded blue djellaba, the traditional Moroccan country dress. Only plastic sandals held together by tape covered her feet. No one would sit next to us. My aunt, Hafeza, who also had money, didn't sit beside us. She positioned herself between two fashionable women whose children whispered and made faces.

The doctor's assistant made us wait for three hours. All the other wealthy patients, even the ones who came in after us, were seen first. Finally, we were herded into the doctor's office. He was a thin man with a pencil mustache and large lips. He sat rigidly behind a large desk and did not attempt to get up when we entered the room. The man had a haughty, arrogant manner.

"Hafeza talked, speaking in French rather than the common Moroccan language. Slowly, she outlined the story of Gabriel's symptoms and his persistent illness. The doctor listened, bored, occasionally tapping the side of his head with his index finger.

When Hafeza reached the point in the story where my mother had stopped breastfeeding, the man suddenly leaped to his feet.

"'You did what?' he roared, glowering at my mother. Quickly, he came around from behind the desk. In one swift movement, he plucked Gabriel from my mother's arms, letting his diaper drop to the floor. He held Gabriel up, hefting the wiggling baby like he was nothing but a sack of potatoes. Holding him out in front of his chest, he gauged his weight and looked at his emaciated arms and legs.

"'I should call the police and have you charged with neglect,' he said to my mother. 'What you've done is nothing short of criminal.'

"Fear spread over my mother's face. She turned to her sister, thinking she would tell the doctor it was her idea. My aunt said nothing.

"Peering at Hafiza's expensive clothes and imperial manner, he made a snap decision. 'The boy is to live with his aunt.' He pointed a finger at my mother. 'Do you understand? You're not a fit mother. From now on, your sister will raise the boy.'

"Hafeza, who had never been able to have children, smiled.

"In those days, the doctor's word was the law. My mother had no choice but to accept his decision. We were poor. My uneducated, illiterate mother couldn't fight her educated sister. On the taxi ride home, Hafeza held Gabriel in her arms. She cooed at him in a soothing voice. My forlorn mother could do nothing. At home, Hafeza pocketed his teddy bear and a few diapers.

"'I'll buy all new things,' she said, looking down her nose at my mother. "'I can provide better for him than you.'

"For the next five years, Gabriel lived with my aunt. She indeed clothed him in expensive clothes and provided fine toys. Her house was elegant and refined. She took him to the South of Morocco each year to stay at a beachfront villa. At that time, Gabriel's older sister, Fatima, was living with Hafeza, working as a maid for my aunt's family. Fatima was actually taking care of Gabriel. She fed him, bathed him, and played with him. In some ways, she acted like his mother.

"My mother's heart ached for the loss of her child. Each Friday, she rode the bus for two hours to see Gabriel. She would hold him close to her heart and rock him for hours. She wanted to spend even more time with her child and sleep with him through the night. Hafeza became jealous and forbade my mother from staying. Gabriel grew used to the fine home, abundant toys, and luxurious surroundings.

"Finally, Hafeza made plans to travel to Iraq to see a close friend. Because she was not Gabriel's real mother, he couldn't travel out of the country with her. My mother saw the opportunity to reclaim her child. She hurried to her sister's house, gathered Gabriel's things, and brought him home.

"For Gabriel, it was a tremendous shock. Gone was the fine home and expensive neighborhood. Hafeza, whom he had come to identify as his mother, was also gone. He had to adapt to a new home and life. It was a life he had to share with five brothers and sisters. Most importantly, he was thrust into a life of verbal abuse and physical beatings from his father."

I spoke to Gabriel a few days after the discussion with his sister. He confirmed Sanaa's account of what had happened during the time with his aunt. He stated that he still regretted being taken from Hafeza.

"Imagine being ripped from a life of privilege and luxury to having to deal with the daily torment my father inflicted upon me," he said.

I nodded silently, watching him on WhatsApp.

"What does this have to do with *Return to Your Heart*?" I asked. We had been discussing this concept. I had suggested that the sessions we were doing together were helping him connect with his heart. "Where is this taking you?"

Gabriel paused. "I have been going deeper, looking more profoundly at my life," he said. "I guess this is something."

Return to Your Heart is the journey to connect more deeply with what we can call our emotional or intuitive heart. It is the essential journey of life. Inner peace, tranquility, and love await the dedicated traveler. Often, however, the journey is stalled. A dense fog clouds the expedition. Like Gabriel, emotional traumas keep us from parting the mist and sever our deep heart connection. Shackled, we are veiled from the inner Divine Light. Remember, I have said that the Divine Light lives within every heart. It is a light of love, mercy, and compassion. Within this brilliant light lies the knowledge of who we are as human beings. We are not the limited self. We have been created from "God stuff"; all the majesty and unlimited possibilities of the Universe course through our arteries and veins.

The Sufis have written, "He who knows Himself knows his Lord."[27] Once we understand that we carry the Light of The Divine within our being, we see ourselves differently. Slowly, the rising waters of shame, guilt, and unworthiness recede. We begin to know ourselves. An airy sense of blessedness infuses our psyche. We feel the light from our Creator pulsating within our hearts. We understand that we are the wave. He is the ocean. Importantly, we are inseparable. This knowledge transforms our view of the world and ourselves. We see ourselves as perfect in our imperfections. Yes, we need work, but the light inside will guide us.

When we want to know real peace and discover the indescribable love within, we must begin living and moving more from our hearts. This is the *Return To Your Heart*. It is a process for engaging people with an open heart, a heart that is willing to give and receive love. Living with an open heart is something we all understand.

We have all come across people who emit a special charisma. We meet them and instantly feel a heart connection, a mysterious expansion in our chest. It's like they are truly "with us." We sense it in the softness of their words, or the bond created when they give us their full attention. The best analogy to explain it is "their heart is holding us." It's the mother's embrace—a feeling of warmth, acceptance, and unconditional love when in the loving mother's presence. We spoke earlier about "the eye of the heart" as the mother's eye for her child. *Return to Your Heart* is the way to look at all people with the deep gaze of a mother. It is an open-hearted embrace. My spiritual guide has that gaze. When I am in his presence, I feel his love for me. It's an overwhelming feeling of being embraced and held in love.

We should not underestimate the power of an open heart in

changing our lives. Dean Ornish, M.D., was the first cardiologist to prove that coronary heart disease could be reversed. Before his groundbreaking research in the 1980s, heart disease was considered an incurable, fatal illness. People were often instructed to get their affairs in order because they had only six months to live—hence the fear of heart disease.

Dr. Ornish developed a unique program for reversing heart disease. He demonstrated that combining diet, exercise, and living with what he called "an open heart" could undo the damaging effects of heart disease.[28] In other words, *their death sentence could be lifted.* Following his guidance, patients were required to actively exercise, eat properly, and do yoga relaxation twice weekly. They were also placed in group therapy and *openheartedness* classes. They were encouraged to explore the deep, emotional issues that troubled their hearts. His unparalleled work proved the importance of a deep heart connection in healing real heart disease.

In *Inner Peace Now,* I have provided a framework for creating a life of open-heartedness. In a later chapter, I will share with you how to *Develop a Daily Heart Connection Practice.* It is an essential skill for emotional, psychological, and spiritual heart healing. As I have outlined, the first step is awareness. We have to be aware that something is wrong in our lives. Like Gabriel, if we are feeling anxiety, emotional pain, or psychic paralysis, we have to be aware and acknowledge that we have a problem. Next, we have to begin the reflection process. Deep reflection comes when we first get relaxed, then we connect to our hearts. Remember, "Ask, and it will be given to you."[29] It is a promise from the All-Loving. If you get quiet and bring your attention to your heart, your heart will respond. In time, utilization of *The Remembrance* practice will cement your deep inner connection to your heart.

Gabriel's experience with heart healing sessions should clarify that focusing on our heart and then using breath and the sound of the Divine Name can create an opening within us. The Divine Name, the electricity of love, penetrates the dark veils of the heart. It shakes them, exposing the negative pictures blocking the flow of love, and, in time, the restrictions of the heart lift.

Once we have become aware and started the reflection process, we have begun the journey that will return us to our hearts. It is a voyage like no other. It is a trip that will allow you to cross the dark and turbulent waters that are pummeling our world. It takes a strong, ocean-going vessel to carry you through these difficult times.

If you suffer from anxiety, fear, or panic attacks or are paralyzed by the difficulties of life, know that the journey to your heart can give you the answers you seek. The Sufis say that *The Path of Love* is the ship that can guide us across the churning waters of life. The waves are so deep that we can lose our way without a sea-worthy vessel, a ship that has made the journey before. Understand that the All-Merciful, All-Compassionate Creator has placed this vessel within us. It is our heart. Our hearts carry the wisdom that can guide us to a place of peace, love, mercy, and compassion. Our work is to travel to the deep heart.

We won't find it in the latest app or television show, alcohol or marijuana. Like Gabriel, we won't find it bar hopping, partying, or chasing romantic partners. All of these close off our hearts. They deaden our senses and cut off the heart connection.

At a deeper level, the return to our hearts is the return to love. For most people, love is an abstract idea. We may love our wives or children, but this kind of love is frequently selfish. Many times, we love something for what it can do for us. If I love my wife only for what she can do for me—cook dinner, take care of the children, provide physical satisfaction—this will not give me what I truly want and need.

Returning to the heart means to return to real, selfless love. It is a love that doesn't need anything in return. It also means we must place love at the center of our actions. Love is not passive. Love is action. Much of what is wrong with the world is that we think love is an emotion. Love is much more. As we said earlier, love, like electricity, is a powerful working force. Love can be how we move in the world, but just feeling love isn't enough—it doesn't move us past the emotional state.

Take this example. A man says he loves a woman. He feels love for her in his heart but takes no action. Does the woman know about the man's love? Perhaps her heart may feel it, but love is more abstract here. The man goes out, buys the woman some flowers, and sends them to her. His action has made the feeling of love real. Perhaps now the man will approach the woman and speak to her. He will tell her beautiful things. Love in action affects the woman. It traverses from abstraction to reality.

On a practical level, the return to the heart is a movement away from the outside toward focusing on the inner life. The Sufis say that the heart has two doors. One door leads to the outside, to the created world. The other door leads inside to the Divine Light, the Divine Presence.

If we want to know real peace, absolute joy, and satisfaction, we need to close the door to the outside and open the inner door. Of course, we can't ignore the outside world. We live and move in this world. But we need to balance our travels through life. Importantly, we need to make the journey to our heart. *The Path of Love* is this journey. It is a way to cross the oceans of difficulty and land on the shore of *Inner Peace Now*.

Begin your journey. Return to Your Heart.

6

EMBRACE SELF-FORGIVENESS

*The most terrifying thing is
to accept oneself completely.*
—CARL JUNG

The summer crept laboriously for Gabriel. Inactivity had fed his illness. He had learned to keep his body busy and his mind occupied. We had discussed this before his next session in July. He remarked that one Friday, while doing errands, he found himself not far from his old job in the downtown area. Casually, he swung by the restaurant. The front door was locked, and in-person dining was still closed. He pressed his face against the big plate glass window in the front of the building and peered inside. He could see people moving in the back.

Food pickup and delivery must still be working, he thought. He was turning to leave when, suddenly, the front door opened. It was his old manager. He must have seen Gabriel staring in through the window.

"How are you doing, Gabriel?" Amir said. He was a tall Indian man with broad shoulders and a thick chest. They had first met at a local gym. Gabriel had acquired his job as a waiter and kitchen helper through his acquaintance with Amir.

"We're going to be opening back up in a few weeks," he said. He looked quizzically at Gabriel. He knew about Gabriel's illness. They had spoken not long after his first trip to the emergency room.

"I'm still having problems," Gabriel told Amir.

"Okay," Amir said, nodding compassionately. "Call me when you're better."

"How did that make you feel?" I asked after we started another session.

He was perched on his couch wearing a blue sweatshirt and sweatpants. It was early on a Saturday in mid-July. The sliding glass door to his left was open. A magnolia tree's broad, waxy leaves could be seen swaying in the breeze near his porch. Yellow morning sunlight played back and forth across his face with the tree's movements.

"It didn't make me feel good," he said. "It reminded me that things are mostly good but sometimes bad. The pains and anxiety are still bothering me." His facial expression radiated concern. His eyebrows pointed downward, and his facial muscles looked strained.

"But are they less?" I asked.

He fidgeted on the couch. He pinched his mouth together in a frustrated expression.

"Yes, they are less. The pain is much less," he said. "I'll go three or four days without any pain or anxiety, but then out of nowhere, I'll awaken in the middle of the night, and the anxiety will be overwhelming. I will be sweating and shaking. It's horrible."

Embrace Self-Forgiveness

I nodded my head in acknowledgment of his pain. "It is often the nature of the healing process that it takes time," I said. "It is like this in every illness. I see it commonly in my cardiology patients. People want things to be over quickly. They grow weary within the walls of an illness. It is written that people are created in haste.[30] It is the culture. We live in the 'now' generation. However, life isn't like this. Life is a process, a movement down a rarely straight road." We had discussed this previously, but I made it clear to him again: Healing takes time.

Gabriel needed to continue down the slow road to inner peace. In his book *Atomic Habits*, best-selling author James Clear writes about the importance of sustained seemingly small habits in delivering success. *"We all face challenges in life. The experience has taught me a critical lesson: changes that seem small and unimportant at first will compound into remarkable results if you're willing to stick with them."*[31] Reflection and practice of *The Remembrance* needed to be stamped into Gabriel's daily routine.

Gabriel also required forgiveness. Indeed, embracing self-forgiveness can be another step that propels us down the *Path of Love*. It is one of the catalysts that speed our inner travel. You may be thinking, "What do I have to forgive? I've done nothing wrong. People have wronged me." Or you may realize, "Yes, I have sometimes hurt others." People come from various intellectual and emotional backgrounds. They have assorted psychological makeups and personalities. If a person lacks awareness, they may be truly unaware if they have wronged others. Not everyone is cognizant of how they live and move in the world. It's safe to say that, most likely, everyone needs forgiveness.

"Let's move deeper into your heart," I said to Gabriel.

We went through the relaxation process of our session

"Put your awareness about three inches beneath the chest wall, where your heart lies. Let yourself go deeper. We continued saying, Ahhh, Ahhh, Ahhh. I watched his face closely for clues to his state. I didn't see any.

"Now I want you to feel into your heart," I said. "Keep your focus in your heart region and tell me what you feel."

I don't feel anything, he said.

"Again, this is not uncommon." I reminded him of an earlier conversation. "In the beginning, when people learn to connect to their hearts, they will not feel anything. The heart has to open. Sometimes it takes a while, a few days or months, to become aware of your heart's feelings. The key is not to judge yourself. Be okay with whatever you get. If you don't get anything, it's all right. If you sense something, trust the first thing that comes to mind."

Examining his expression, I could see it was flat and calm but without emotion. His body posture was medium, not tense or overly limp.

"Some people never get anything," I said soothingly. "Just be okay with whatever you feel. Don't judge yourself. Let come what comes."

I continued to breathe out *The Remembrance,* pushing it toward him and almost singing the words. Next, I asked him to imitate my cadence of *The Remembrance.* We breathed deeply and exhaled the Ahhh, letting it work its way down into his heart.

"Now, what do you feel?" I asked after forty seconds.

"I'm starting to see something," he said. His voice was

hushed like he was examining, waiting for a pattern to form. "It's in the clouds like the clouds are starting to part." I stared at his face, a quizzical expression forming.

"Okay, I'm back with my sister, Sarah," he said. "She's sitting in the salon. She has some prayer beads. She's saying something over and over."

"What is she saying?" I asked.

"She's saying. 'I'm a good girl. I'm a good girl.'"

A guttural sound came from Gabriel's throat. He was choking back his tears.

"I'm afraid I'll be all alone," he said. His crying became louder, and tears started to run down his face.

"Let's go back to *The Remembrance*," I said. "Let *The Remembrance* flow into the pictures of your heart."

"Ahhh, Ahhh, Ahhh," we said the words together. His crying subsided.

"Why are you afraid of being alone?" I asked. "You have your brother; you have your family. Why are you afraid?" I reminded him that this feeling had surfaced in an earlier session.

"I don't know," he said. "I'm just afraid."

We returned to *The Remembrance*, letting the combination of sound and breath wash his heart. I said, "Now take a very deep breath, and then when you exhale, let the Ahhh penetrate into the picture. Feel it as light and love." He continued like this until the crying was completely gone and the sadness left his face.

"Now, I want you to call to your Creator," I said. "I want you to ask your heart or your Creator, Why am I afraid of being alone? What is my real fear?"

I was quiet, watching as his chest moved in and out deeply. I let some time pass, waiting for his answer. "What do you feel?" I asked eventually.

"I've been bad. I've done things I shouldn't have done," he said. He pursed his lips together. An expression of judgment racked his face.

"What things?" I asked.

"I can't tell. I'm too embarrassed. I'm ashamed," he said

"Not to worry, you don't need to share them with me. Now ask your heart another question," I said softly. "What does this have to do with your fear of being alone? How are they connected?"

He said nothing. After a few minutes, we returned to *The Remembrance*.

"Did you get anything?" I asked.

"No," he replied.

We returned to the opener, *The Remembrance* of the Divine Name. We used it even more strongly, sending it further into the heart, like the electricity of love; its sound was almost palpable.

"Now what do you feel?" I asked gently.

A look of fear had flashed over his face. His limbs were tense.

"I'm afraid God won't forgive me for my sins," he said. "I'm afraid that when I die, all my sins will send me to hell. I'll be alone, truly alone."

A piercing shriek came out of his mouth, a cry like a caged animal. Next, he moaned loudly and struggled back and forth on the couch. He clutched his face with both of his hands. Soon, a torrent of tears flowed, streaking down to the corners of his mouth. I toned *The Remembrance* as he sobbed over and over.

Embrace Self-Forgiveness

"I didn't help my sister. She died alone. I was a man. I didn't stop my father from beating her and my mother. I'm a man. I'm a man, and I didn't stop him," he said, weeping.

Over and over for many minutes, his body shook with spasms of anguish, grief, and words of hopelessness.

"You couldn't do anything," I said.

We revisited an earlier conversation. By the time Gabriel reached seventeen years old, he had grown into manhood. He was bigger than his father and stronger. After one ferocious beating where his father had grabbed his mother's head and smashed it into the floor, Gabriel and his brother pleaded with their mother to let them "teach their father a lesson." "We'll give him a beating as he gave you." Even with her face inflamed from his blows and her eyes black and blue, his mother shook her finger at them. "No, it will just make things worse. He'll throw us all out into the street." Hadiya had been an orphan. She knew the desperate life that awaited a homeless family in Morocco. She feared that none of her relatives would take them in, and they would become beggars on the street. She counseled the brothers to remain calm and avoid confrontation with their father. Gabriel loved his mother deeply, so he had to honor her wishes despite the disastrous results. They didn't intervene. Year after year, the abuse continued. Gabriel, Jacob, and the remaining sisters eventually migrated to foreign countries to escape the continual terror. Hadiya stayed, and she suffered.

When Hadiya reached retirement age, her husband would not let her retire. He retired at sixty, as required by his government job. Her husband forced her to continue working. She trudged three miles up and down hills each morning to a privately run orphanage. She prepared and cooked meals for the one hundred children who lived at the facility. It was a physically challenging job, carrying huge pots of food from the kitchen over to the mess hall. Afterward, she was required to clean all the dishes, most often by herself.

Meanwhile, Gabriel's father had inherited a large farm in the south of Morocco, near Marrakech. During planting season, Hadiya was forced to travel with him to the farm, where his father had hired ten employees to plant the fields and care for the sheep.

Hadiya was the cook and the maid. Before dawn, she trekked out into the wild part of the farm. Often, she walked nearly a mile as she scavenged enough firewood and kindling. She carried the heavy firewood draped over her shoulder in a large canvas sack.

Hadiya would be slapped or punched if breakfast wasn't ready before the men awoke. As she grew older, the years of excruciating work and physical abuse took a toll on her health.

When he was seventy, Gabriel's father asked Hadiya for permission to take a second wife, which was permitted in Morocco. He didn't want a divorce. He wanted Hadiya to stay around and work like a slave, cooking, cleaning, and using her meager salary for food. He would bring a younger woman into the home who could work more. When Hadiya refused this arrangement, he tried beating Hadiya into submission. Day after day, he physically and verbally abused her. After one terrible thrashing, where he blackened both her eyes and knocked her unconscious, her children convinced her it was time to escape. Two of his sisters flew to Morocco, and they spirited her away in the dark of the night. Soon, his father went to the courts and divorced his mother. He took all her possessions and even stole her inheritance of land.

"I should have done something," Gabriel said. Bitterness tinged his voice.

"It wasn't your fault," I said consolingly.

Now the emotional cause of his illness was clear. A fault line of shame and feelings of dishonor had been exposed. Gabriel was afraid that God wouldn't forgive him for not listening and following what his heart urged him to do. He feared living and dying alone.

"Come back to *The Remembrance*," I said to Gabriel. "Return to your heart."

Softly, he began sounding his Sacred Name for God. His crying abated. Within a few moments, his pain and sadness subsided. We waited some time as he lay in silence. When his composure returned, I asked him to open his eyes and sit up. I watched as he slowly responded.

"How do you feel now?" I asked.

He took a deep breath, shaking off the emotional tension coursing through his body. He checked himself for a few seconds.

"I'm not sure," he said, hesitating. He swiveled his head slowly back and forth. His eyes drifted over his body, doing a mental check. "Okay, I think." He shook his limbs and readjusted himself on the couch.

"What do you make of what we discovered today?" I asked.

A pensive expression plodded over his face.

"I never would have imagined that the fear and panic I feel now relates to me being afraid that God wouldn't forgive me for what I did in regard to my mother. In my conscious mind, I know I've done nothing wrong. I couldn't have helped Sarah, and my mother wouldn't let me intervene in her marriage. It seems odd that the anxiety and pain that I feel would bring all this up," he said.

"Remember, the trauma we hold in our hearts isn't rational. It's a child's memory, an adolescent's thinking," I said.

"Right, I know that in here," he said, tapping his head. "But it's strange that I've held on to that all my life."

"Yes, but don't forget. Our hearts veil the painful emotional traumas of our lives. But they are waiting to be released. Their hold on you will diminish once they are identified. Your heart will begin to open. More love can begin flowing into your heart and nourishing your body. You've started walking down the *Path of Love*. It takes a while."

We spent some time talking about forgiveness. I asked Gabriel to begin reflecting on how he could start forgiving himself for the feelings that had been discovered. He needed to ponder these things, ask his heart for guidance, and call on his Creator to let him accept the forgiveness that his heart needed.

We agreed to meet in a few weeks, depending on his feelings.

What do we need to forgive? The best forgiveness begins with us. We need to be willing to offer ourselves the gentle hand of forgiveness. Why? Why would we need to forgive ourselves? Many people like Gabriel hold onto guilt about the mistakes and missteps they have made in life. Guilt can be a powerful force that disturbs our hearts. It can separate and immobilize the psyche.

In my own experience of doing hundreds of healing sessions—self-loathing, self-anger, and guilt are common emotions that prevent a person from finding lasting happiness—people judge themselves harshly. They find it hard to let go of self-recrimination. Their mental images of themselves conjure ugliness, even hatred. It's an entangling web that wraps itself inside like an evil spell. It whispers injuriously *You're no good. You're not worthy of being loved.* We need to be gentle with ourselves for not having lived and moved in the best possible way.

Here is the first forgiveness. We must forgive ourselves. We must speak with ourselves and ask our own hearts for forgiveness. We must let ourselves off the hook and stop beating ourselves up for not doing what we should have done.

We must claim our humanness. We are all human. We make mistakes. We need to recognize that no human being can be perfect. None of us can always be loving. None of us is Divine. We are the created. We are not the Creator. My teacher Shayk Ninowy has said, "I am only perfect in my imperfections."

Forgiving ourselves isn't always easy. One of my students, a beautiful and incredibly caring woman, has struggled to embrace self-forgiveness. She's in her late forties with long, raven hair stippled with strands of gray. Her smile is quick, and she has an even quicker wit. But her conservative Christian upbringing molded her with a view of God as vengeful and punishing in His severity. Her skewed image of her Creator left her constantly thinking she was a *bad* person. That she didn't deserve the mercy and love that came her way in life. The concept of self-forgiveness was foreign.

Amazingly, over the last twelve years, she has performed *The Remembrance* daily and pulled and pushed her heart down the journey to inner peace. And the All-Loving, Most-Merciful has poured His magical elixir of love onto her life. The spider's web of ill thoughts and beliefs about herself has receded. They are not gone, but their tenacles are less sticky.

Another powerful way to embrace self-forgiveness is to ask forgiveness from a power higher than ourselves. The All-Forgiving, All-Loving Creator is the ultimate power of the universe. He is the true forgiver. If we are willing, we should call to our Creator and ask for forgiveness for any mistakes we think we have made. We can ask forgiveness for not living entirely in love. With this, a true revelation can emerge. When we acknowledge that a power greater than ourselves exists—a loving, forgiving being—the heart can connect back to the inner light even more fully.

The key is to ask for forgiveness and accept that we have been forgiven. Like the woman I just mentioned, it may be difficult. Often, we have no trouble asking for forgiveness, but accepting that our missteps have been absolved is another issue altogether.

We need to understand that the All-Loving *wants* to forgive us. He is the Forgiver. He hears your pleadings, and He answers them. Let forgiveness wash the guilt and shame from your heart. Know that acceptance of your forgiveness is instantaneous. In the blink of an eye, all mistakes are erased.

Embracing self-forgiveness can open the door to a richer and fuller life. Self-recrimination can take a toll on our psyches. It can make us feel unworthy, even despicable. Such self-doubt and internal judgment hinder our ability to enjoy life. Embracing

Embrace Self-Forgiveness

self-forgiveness is also a way to move from the problematic outer world and to learn to live more subtly. The inner life is a world of light where peace is the currency. In your time of reflection, begin contemplating. Start the process of forgiving yourself. Acknowledge that you are not perfect. You are indeed imperfect in your imperfection.

Embrace self-forgiveness. It can be a powerful catalyst for your heart's transformation.

7

EXTEND FORGIVENESS TO OTHERS

To forgive is to set a prisoner free and discover that the prisoner was you.
—LEWIS B SMEDES

Gabriel's next session came a month after his previous session. His homework was unchanged—to continue his daily practice of *The Remembrance* and develop the habit of daily reflection. I contacted him on *WhatsApp* because I needed to start earlier on our work together. I caught him as he was sitting in a lawn chair out on the balcony of his apartment. It was an overcast day. Diffuse light crept through the bright green magnolia leaves. We started first with a long conversation about his progress.

"I've been working on the concept of trying to forgive myself," he said. "I still feel a great deal of guilt. I'm not sure I have convinced myself that I am forgivable."

"Yes, learning to accept our own forgiveness can be slow," I said. As an analogy of how progress can be slow, I told him a story of my attempts to walk up a steep hill near my house outside Atlanta, Georgia. It's a mile long with a one-thousand-foot rise. I make the walk right after a long day's work in the summer. The temperature will still be hovering in the nineties with shirt-sticking humidity. It's a tedious climb in the broiling sun. I put one foot in front of the other, step by step. Slowly, imperceptibly, I crawl upward. I keep my head down, not wanting to discourage myself with my sluggish progress by looking up. Finally, after what seems like forever, I reach the summit. Only then can I raise my head and see what I have accomplished.

"Accepting our self-forgiveness is like this climb," I said. "It seems like we'll never make it until we look up and are there."

"Well, I haven't reached the top of that hill," he said.

He had moved inside the apartment and was now settled on the couch. I watched his movements closely. His facial expression was neither angry nor worried. No fear moved across his face. His posture was also neutral. He displayed no signs of hidden tension.

"Why do you think that is?" I asked.

He shrugged his shoulders, lifting his hand palm upward. "I don't know," he said.

I explained to him that people raised in very conservative religious cultures commonly hold tightly to the idea of a vengeful, judging God. Often, they have a strong sense of unworthiness and sinfulness. Far too frequently, guilt is welded like an emotional hammer to have children strictly follow their rules and develop good behavior habits. It can be a strong motivational tool.

Similar feelings can be fostered in people raised with very judgmental parents. Feelings of unworthiness fester inside their hearts. Their minds may know they are *good* people, but, subconsciously, they feel they are evil and unworthy of forgiveness. It often takes a long time, with a strong reinforcement of the fact that the All-Mighty is indeed the Most Loving and the Most Merciful, for them to shed these inner convictions.

I spent a few minutes relaying the understanding that The All-Merciful has embedded his love within us. We are made of *God stuff,* powerful forces of light and love.

"Does that make sense to you?" I asked.

He nodded again. "Sure, it makes sense mentally," he said. "I am aware of this concept. I believe it in my mind, but I'm not sure my heart is convinced."

"We'll need to continue working on that," I said. "Do you have any other issues that have been coming up?"

"Contemplating about forgiveness brought up some other issues that have bothered me," he said. He related a story about how he was hurt emotionally in his previous job. At that time, he was working as a dishwasher and clean-up man in the restaurant.

He had befriended one of the young women near his age, Jean, who worked at the restaurant too. In their conversations, he had confided in her about a time when he had gotten close to another woman named Sheila. Sheila was a blond woman with bright blue eyes who seemed to want a romantic relationship. One day, however, they were walking and holding hands while doing some shopping at a mall. Suddenly, she dropped his hand and moved a few feet away from him. They continued to walk apart from each other until they came upon a few of her friends. She acted like she hardly knew him. When he questioned her about why she had dropped his hand and moved away from him, she said it was because of his dark skin color. She didn't want her friends to see her walking in that way with a man who wasn't white. He was devastated. America, he had thought, wasn't a racist society. He believed it to be color blind. Unfortunately, the color of his skin did matter, at least to Sheila. It had been quite the blow. It had taken him many months to recover from the ache inside his heart.

And he hadn't recovered. The pain still festered deep within his psyche. Rather than acknowledge it, he had pushed it below the surface. He had locked it away. It was too painful to pull out of his inner safe place and examine. He couldn't muster the emotional strength. It was too painful to consider how a person could judge him for the color of his skin, could see him as something less than she saw herself—another human being. Didn't all of us come from one soul, the soul of Adam? How could a person not look past the outside to really see him?

He told Jean about the incident, sharing his feelings of pain and rejection with her. A couple days later, he was working at the restaurant, and one of his co-workers, whom he didn't get along with, came up to him and said, "I hear the white women don't want anything to do with you because you're too dark." Apparently, Jean had been gossiping about his difficulty to her co-workers. The man's jab had rekindled the flame of anger inside him. Over and over, he relived the event. It was like being betrayed a second time.

Gabriel revealed to me that this incident brought up tremendous anger and distrust. For years, he had been unable to overcome this betrayal and had been unwilling to confide in anyone except his family members. The episode only reinforced his fear of opening his heart.

"I know we have been discussing the concept of self-forgiveness," I said. "But have you ever considered the idea of extending your forgiveness further? What do you think about the idea of forgiving these two women who betrayed your trust?"

Gabriel paused. He gazed downward, thinking silently.

"Forgiving them for what they did to me?" he said, slowly shaking his head sideways. He paused a second time. "They were in the wrong. Where's the justice in that? They're the ones who should be asking for forgiveness, not me." His jaw set tightly and he looked me straight in the eye. "I did nothing wrong."

"Yes," I said, "that's true. Justice is on your side. But clearly, their betrayal still troubles you. Realize that forgiving them doesn't condone their actions. What they did was wrong. Forgiveness doesn't get them off the hook for their cruel actions, but it could help you."

"Help me?" he asked. "I don't see how forgiving them can help me much." His posture was rigid on the couch. Strained lines of tension creased his face.

"Well, clearly, you're still hurt and angry. Negative feelings like this can damage your health," I said.

"What do you mean?" he asked.

Slowly, I began discussing why extending forgiveness to others is crucial. Robert Enright, Ph.D., in his book *Eight Keys to Forgiveness*, says that "forgiveness can save your life. None of us wants to waste time when it comes to our healing. Sometimes, life hits us so hard that our options narrow when finding healing for the blow. I have never found anything as effective as forgiveness for healing deep wounds."[32] I've included a link to a video that outlines this concept (https://youtu.be/gdgPAetNY5U?si=_gxdm6APNDEVEKAC)

Dr. Enright outlines numerous medical studies showing why forgiveness is essential for ideal health. One particularly compelling study demonstrated that forgiveness therapy could improve blood flow in people with blocked coronary heart arteries. These were patients who had undergone a cardiac nuclear stress test (an advanced method for evaluating whether a person has coronary heart blockages). Their tests demonstrated regions of their heart muscle with diminished blood flow. Patients like this are at a much higher risk of having a heart attack. Their blood flow improved after ten weeks of forgiveness therapy. Most cardiologists would conclude that their risk of a heart attack was also reduced.[33] Dr. Enright's claim that forgiveness can save your life isn't an overstatement.

Indeed, learning how to forgive others has other benefits. It can help a person reduce their anxiety. His research showed that people in a drug rehabilitation program who felt they had been treated harshly had a significant anxiety reduction back to normal.[34] His work has shown other improvements in health: increased focus, decreased symptoms of PTSD, increased feelings of self-esteem, and even a feeling of improvement in quality of life.[35] What's more, extending forgiveness to others is essential for releasing the feelings of anger that boil inside of us.

Gabriel understood such anger. His resentment and bitterness toward these two women smoldered within his heart.

Extend Forgiveness to Others

He possessed similar feelings for his father. The years of abuse had left him feeling raw and wounded. Forgiveness for his father would not come easily.

After this lengthy discussion, it was time to proceed.

"Let's move deeper into your heart," I said to Gabriel. "Let's start today's healing session," I asked him to recline back on the couch. He laid his head back and slumped downward.

"Do you feel relaxed?" I asked him.

"Yes, I'm comfortable and feel calm," he said.

We moved through the series of relaxation exercises and the heart-focusing method. Next, we launched into two to three minutes of *The Remembrance*. I observed Gabriel's countenance. His arms were lying limp, folded over his lower abdomen. I could see no stress on his face.

"What are you feeling inside your heart?" I asked him.

He gauged this heart quietly. His reply was monotone: "Nothing. It's calm," he said.

I made a conscious effort to put my awareness into my heart. I opened my heart. I set the intention to expand my heart and let it envelop Gabriel. A feeling of deeper calmness came over me. We returned to *The Remembrance* together for another four minutes. I raised the timbre of my voice and made it melodious. I watched as his breathing slowed and deepened. The muscles of his face became serene.

"Now, I would like you to consider forgiving the two women who betrayed you. Just let this idea sink into your heart," I said. As he did this, I lowered the volume of my voice, returning to my *Remembrance*. I let this go for a minute or two.

"Now, what are you feeling?" I asked. I could see something happening to his facial expression. His eyes were still closed, and he looked like he was peering into what I imagined to be a dark, foggy night. I went back to the Ahhh, Ahhh, Ahhh.

"I can see them both. I can hear our conversations. I remember everything word for word just like they spoke it to me," he said. A few seconds passed. "My heart is starting to become tight. It's like a lump is forming inside my chest. It is red and jittery. I'm angry. I'm very angry at both of them."

"Keep your focus on that area of anger. Please say Ahhhh directly into the lump. It's like you will send the Ahhh in the form of love and let it penetrate the anger. Say it out loud. Do that now," I said. I listened to his voice. It was soft, but I could see it vibrating his chest. I began saying Ahhh as well, merging with his voice. We continued this for three minutes, then I paused. "Now, what do you feel?" I asked.

"The anger is gone," he said.

"Good. What about your feelings of hurt or betrayal?" I asked. I watched his facial expression. He didn't seem angry. No anguish simmered on the surface. He had a quizzical expression as if he was trying to make sense of things.

"I can feel their hearts. It's like they think they are better than me," he said. He paused again, sorting out his feelings. "I'm no longer angry at them, but I feel sad. I think they are insecure. They get some pleasure out of thinking they are better than others. However, I think they know what they are doing is wrong." His voice was steady and calm. Gabriel shifted on the couch.

"Let's go back to *The Remembrance* together," I said. "Once more, try to take the sound and breathe directly into that part of your heart that contains these pictures." I began a slow cadence of Ahhh, Ahhh, Ahhh, I pulsed it like musical beats into his heart. His voice followed mine. I watched as his chest rose and fell rhythmically. We continued with this for some time.

"Now, what is your heart feeling?" I asked.

Once again, his face was filled with a searching expression. I softly murmured *The Remembrance,* delicate notes of vibratory love projected toward him. I waited.

"My heart is more open to them. I'm not sure I can forgive them, but I don't see them as evil anymore. I think they're flawed people. They've done me wrong. It was shameful how they treated me," he said, pausing as he let this awareness diffuse through his being. "But I don't feel hatred toward them anymore. It's gone."

I asked him to open his eyes and sit up. Gabriel repositioned himself on the couch as he stroked his chin.

"How do you feel?" I asked.

"Better. I feel less angry at them now," he said, nodding. "I still don't understand how they could treat me this way."

"Yes, understanding how people can be mean and treat people unjustly is difficult to fathom," I said. "But it's good that your anger is less."

How do you start the process of *Extending Forgiveness to Others*?

First, you need to become clear about why forgiving others is essential. Your physical and emotional health will likely improve if you forgive the people who have hurt you. You are not letting them off the hook for their harmful actions. They don't have free reign to hurt you again. Forgiveness is not weakness or capitulation. Enright writes, "Suppose you see forgiveness as 'just moving on.' Many see forgiveness this way, but it is not correct. You can 'move on' with great resentment in your heart, which will hardly germinate hope, love, strength, and joy within you. Forgiveness must be much more than 'moving on.' True forgiveness must lighten our hearts and foster inner peace."[36]

A companion task for achieving forgiveness is to commit to and choose love over resentment and bitterness. All too often, we want to hold onto our hurtful memories. We replay them in endless inner loops, wallowing in their mud. It's like we want our hurt. We need to relive it and not forget it. And we couple this with the desire for revenge. Our pain is often so acute, so strong that we want our assaulter to experience some of the misery that troubles us. But revenge, resentment, and bitterness won't heal us. Only love can heal such wounds.

The second step of *Extending Forgiveness to Others* is to look at the perpetrator in a different, softer light. We must move past blame and gaze again with the eye of the heart, the loving eye. Such a movement isn't easy, but no one is all evil or all good. All of us carry positive and negative qualities. Sometimes, *we* do things that injure others. We don't always know what we are doing. The person who has harmed us emotionally is also a complex individual. Often, fear and insecurity drive their actions. They may have personality flaws created in their childhood that make them unable to love. Their harmful actions could reflect learned behavior. Once again, this is not to condone their action, but real forgiveness demands that we operate at a much higher level. It is an attempt to offer an unfathomable love called *mercy*.

Mercy is love offered to a person who doesn't deserve it. A person who has battered us unjustly, emotionally or physically, and hasn't acknowledged their error demonstrates a lack of respect, compassion, and fairness. Their attitude suggests that they think of themselves as better than others. All people are made from one soul and carry the divine image inside.

When we give mercy, we engage people with a high form of love. We are offering a love that seems to defy logic. Mercy asks us to ignore the sticks and stones they hurled at us. When you give mercy, you are giving what wasn't given to you. It's essential to recognize that we are not looking to make amends. We are not reconciling with the other person. Our first attempt at mercy is us offering them a gift of love. We don't ask for anything in return. Reconciliation generally comes much later. Reconciliation is a two-way street that can only come with the willingness of both parties. It is a negotiation process of arriving at mutual trust. When we forgive through mercy, we consciously decide to love a person who has unfairly harmed us. It is a one-way giving of love.

My spiritual teacher, Muhammad ar-Rifa'i, tells a story illustrating reaching out through *mercy*. In his book, *Music of the Soul*, he tells the story of a disgruntled man. He and his two young sons would come each day, jeering and literally throwing stones at Muhammad ar-Rifa'i's school in Damascus. Month after month, the students at the school would have to listen to their taunts and run from their rocks. Eventually, my teacher went to the head of the school. He complained about the "bad man" who was desecrating their holy place. He asked *his* teacher what they could do to stop the man. The spiritual master looked at him, smiling, and, with a slight nod of his head, told him to do nothing. The rock-throwing continued unabated. Finally, after several more months, the protests stopped. Soon after, the spiritual master told his student to take food and check on the man. When Muhammad knocked on his door and checked on the man, he found him lying, very sick, in bed. The man said, "Who are you?"

"It's Muhammad from the school." He told him that he had come to help him. The "bad man" looked at him and began crying. For many weeks, my teacher cared lovingly for the man. Eventually, the man became well and came to study at the school, and he started his spiritual journey down the *Path of Love*.

Years later, Muhammad al-Jamal came across the man again; he was now a spiritual teacher.

Muhammad asked, "Why did you throw stones at the school?"

The man replied, "If I hadn't thrown stones, I would never have walked the path and come to know real love."[37]

This story illustrates that deep wisdom often lies behind challenging aspects of our lives. We may want to lash out or seek revenge when people malign us. However, giving mercy is usually the better course of action.

We shouldn't think that offering forgiveness to those who have abused us is always easy. It isn't. Sure, forgiving someone who has done something we find mildly unjust—such as cutting in front of us at a grocery line—might not be that challenging.

Extend Forgiveness to Others

But forgiving more profound abuse, such as Gabriel forgiving his father, often proves to be more challenging.

You may want to start working on daily forgiveness if you constantly find yourself angry or perplexed, even with small slights. By this, I mean using your reflection time to identify the issues causing your dismay and then applying my first two steps. Look to see if you can empathize with the person you feel has wronged you. Try to look at them through the lens of love and mercy. Once you have become more forgiving of small hurts, graduate to identifying more substantial ones. The book *Eight Keys to Forgiveness* offers several practical mental exercises for facilitating this process.

My methods are directed more at the heart level. Heart work can accelerate the process of healing. Opening our hearts to forgive people who have harmed us more substantially brings us to the next step. It requires what I call *Creating a Deeper Container of Love*.

Imagine your heart as a container, a cooking pot. Inside this pot, you have poured a magic elixir of love. If you drop a piece of hurt, a dollop of slight, or a spoonful of pain into your pot, your elixir of love will flow around it. Like magic, the love will slowly embrace these hurts. It will knead and smooth them out until they finally dissolve. But what happens if your container of love is too small? A massive rock of anguish falls on your container, failing to fit entirely within. Your liquid salve of love is now too small to assuage the agony. Attempting to forgive overwhelming hurts can create such difficulty. The trauma may be too significant for our heart's container.

Only by expanding the size of our container can we solve this problem. The steps I have outlined in this book will allow your container to grow. The beginning is looking with the deep eye of a mother's love and trying to empathize with the person who perpetrated your injury. Next, stretch and expand your heart through the continual practice of *The Remembrance*. Finally, ask the All-Loving, All-Merciful Creator to open your heart and ease your heart's pain. Ask for an overwhelming river of love to nourish and sustain you. Soon, your heart will soften, and the mercy you wish to give will pour out of your heart.

If you are still having difficulty or your pain is just too much, I encourage you to seek professional help. Please refer to the disclaimer at the beginning of this book.

Even a small movement toward offering mercy and forgiveness can lessen your heart's pain. Forgiving is just that—a process. It doesn't happen overnight. Months and sometimes years of work may be required. Importantly, the techniques of *The Remembrance* and moving deeper down a *Path of Love* can accelerate your journey.

Remember, the All-Loving, All-Merciful has pulled you into this orbit. Roll up your sleeves. Don't be faint of heart. A life you can't imagine is waiting. Now is your time. Take your chance.

8

PRACTICING GRATITUDE

I am happy because I'm grateful. I choose to be grateful. That gratitude allows me to be happy.
—WILL ARNETT

In addition to the healing powers of awareness, reflection, *The Remembrance,* and opening to forgiveness, I would like to share with you another tool for opening and healing your heart. It is called *practicing gratitude.*

Our hearts are like roses, sweet, dazzling flowers. When a rose is closed, its succulent fragrance is trapped inside. Only when the petals unfold can their amazing scent be experienced. Being grateful and thanking the All-Compassionate Creator for all the blessings shown upon us is the means to open the rose of our hearts. Our thanking needs to be done often; daily is best. A sacred book relates that the All-Mighty has said, "If you are grateful, I will surely grant you increase."[38]

The All-Loving desires our petition of thankfulness. When He says he will grant us an increase, his bounty is infused into our lives on many levels. First, abundance flows to us on the outer material plane. Our outer needs—for clothes, food, and other material necessities—cascade upon us. More importantly, He will increase our deep movement into the heart. Constant thankfulness unleashes the inner fragrance of love. Peace and calmness begin bubbling to the surface of our lives. Often, we feel an expansion within the chest.

If you aren't in the habit of practicing gratitude or haven't tapped into this powerful medicine for the heart, you might be unclear about how to practice this skill. Practicing gratitude means that we sit quietly and examine our lives. We peer with the inner eye, the eye of the heart, searching for those things that the All-Loving has showered down upon us without our asking. Everything good in our lives can prompt us to be grateful. Every person has a different list of the things that are important in their lives. This can be your gratitude list. If you don't have a list or can't think of anything that stirs your heart to feel gratitude, let me give you some suggestions.

First, we need to be grateful for every breath that we take. We need to give thanks for just being alive. Life is like rain. People who live in the desert know this exquisitely. Without rain, nothing grows. Because we are alive, we can love and be loved. It is the power that allows us to work, produce, and enjoy. The gift of life is our most precious gift. Without life, you would be in the ground and moving to another existence. When you create your "I'm grateful for" list, stick "I'm grateful for being alive" at the top of that list, and truly be thankful. Allow yourself to feel the gratitude. Slow down your life. Let the gratitude nurture and open the inner rose of your heart.

A second important item to place on our "I'm grateful for"

Practicing Gratitude

list is the gift of awareness. We can choose to be grateful just for being aware. The Sufis say that *everything is in the love,* meaning that everything about you comes from the blueprint of love that has been delicately positioned inside your heart by the All-Knowing.[39] It sits silently inside the mountain of your heart, waiting to blossom. Why are you reading this book at this moment in your life? Just as Gabriel said, "Why Me? Why Now?" The Sufis say that even your desire to *be* aware comes from the All-Loving's hand. Another saying is, "Nothing hits you that could have missed you,"[40] meaning that the All-Loving's hand is guiding everything. He instills the yearning for self-discovery into a person's heart. Just as all love originates from the Divine source, awareness is another Divine gift. Once we have woken up and understood that we are carriers of the Divine Light, the world becomes our oyster. We can choose to make the journey to our own heart and experience the brilliance of the inner Divine light. Such an awareness demands gratitude. Be grateful that the All-Mighty has opened the door for you to learn this teaching.

And if you choose to move through this book, *Inner Peace Now*, most people will experience a physical sense of heart-opening. A peace that cannot be described with human words will mysteriously begin to swell within your heart. Your heart will soften magically. You'll cry at movies you've never cried at before. The slightest thing—a child's sharp laugh, a bird's fluttering wings on a tree branch, the glint of the sun moving through dark clouds—will stir your heart with incredible love to the point that you think you'll burst. The more you give yourself to *The Remembrance,* the more you will begin to feel it lifting and nourishing your heart. What will be happening is that the eye of your heart is being roused, awoken from its deep slumber.

The journey to your heart awaits. If you are suffering from panic, fear, or inner pain, take hold of the handles of gratitude. Not gratitude of the lips, words that you just say. No, you must embrace gratitude with your heart and your whole being. Each day, when you wake up, search your heart and mind and find something you truly feel thankful for. Be grateful that you have food for breakfast to eat. Acknowledge, thankfully, that you have a bed or mat to sleep on and a roof over your head. Do your children make your heart sing? Does seeing your spouse lighten your face with a smile? Are you happy to have a job and a way to pay your bills? Every day, try to find something that touches your heart with its beauty and simplicity. When you find it, offer the Universe a thank you.

Remember the message, "If you call. I respond."[41] It is a promise from the All-Compassionate giver of life. Once we have been offering thanks and practicing gratitude regularly, we can leap even further into the ocean of the heart. We can begin exploring the idea of *starting to thank our Creator for sucking us into the vortex of swirling, tumultuous difficulty and anguish.* These paralyzing storms of life—pandemics, natural disasters, physical illness, anxiety, depression, financial catastrophes, divorce—all the tragedies that upend our lives, we can closely contemplate these events and *give thanks.* Please understand that the idea of thanking our Creator for such immense difficulty is very, very challenging. It might seem impossible. But it can be done. The simple step of examining such a concept and not tossing this book aside means that your soul is moving deeper.

Let me tell you a story to illustrate this truth. Many years ago, I worked as a cardiologist in a group of twenty-three cardiologists in a Midwestern city. We were the main teaching group for a large university training physicians to be cardiologists. One of the group's cardiologists disliked me strongly. He constantly talked behind my back, telling our cardiology trainees hurtful and untrue things about me. He was overbearing, petty, and condescending toward me.

After many years of this abuse, I began to resent and truly dislike him. I complained bitterly to my friends, who knew his actions were wrong. After a few years, I became fed up with the constant abuse. The final straw was when he tried to have me fired because of preposterous complaints from a mentally ill woman that had been made nine years earlier. Feeling disgusted and worn out by his unprofessional behavior, I left the practice and moved to another state. Inside my heart, I harbored deep feelings of anger that bordered on hatred. If you had asked me at the time if I could see that difficulty as a gift, I would have said, "No way." It was an impossible idea. You could never have convinced me that my Creator was *blessing* me through such heartache. How could such a traumatizing time be a gift?

Fortunately, my move to a new job and state had many positive results. My daily work schedule and weekend on-call time were far less demanding. I reduced my job hours and had every Thursday afternoon and Friday off. The stress level I felt in practicing cardiology was significantly reduced. In addition, I was led to a new spiritual guide who lived in Atlanta, the city where I had moved. Under his tutelage, I soon walked down *The Path of Love* much more profoundly.

After a few years away from the painful memories of my time in the Midwest, I began reflecting on how my life had improved because of that challenging time. I started entertaining the idea that I should be grateful for what had previously happened. If that other cardiologist hadn't badly mistreated me, I would never have gathered the courage and motivation to leave. In my old practice, a cardiologist couldn't reduce their work schedule. If they wanted a reduction in hours, they were forced to retire. No one there had every Friday off, and they still labored for twelve hours each weekend day that they worked at the major hospital. During the week, their schedules were sometimes horrendous.

In time, I began opening my heart to the notion that I should be grateful for what had happened. I started reflecting deeply on the subject. As I looked with the eye of my heart, I could see The All-Merciful's hand moving beneath the surface of that experience. Eventually, I was truly able to be thankful that The All-Loving had allowed me to be swept up by that painful hurricane. My life's beauty and greater ease wouldn't have been possible otherwise. Becoming genuinely thankful soon lifted the anger that had scarred my heart.

As I related in the first chapter of this book, the loving guidance of our Creator is moving through the upheavals that shake our world. He is sending us a message. Looking for love within extreme difficulty is a powerful way to unlock the love within our hearts. If we can summon the inner grace and courage to open our hearts to this idea, we will have turned a corner in our lives.

Gabriel sat comfortably on his couch for our next Zoom meeting. It had been about five months since I started working with him. During this time, he had embraced *The Remembrance* and utilized it for fifteen minutes to half an hour each morning preferably before dawn. In addition, he would use it whenever fear or panic attacks overtook him. These had lessened, and his chest pain had nearly evaporated. No further jaunts to his primary care physician had been necessary, and he hadn't needed to go to the emergency room. In his own words, "Life was seventy-five percent better."

It was time to take the leap of gratitude. Gabriel needed to let go of old, limiting ideas about the nature of life and throw off the opinions that most of us have about suffering and loss.

The Catholic monk and psychologist Thomas Moore, Ph.D., has written eloquently about this in his book *Dark Nights of the Soul.*

"At one time or another, most people go through a period of sadness, trial, loss, frustration, or failure that is so disturbing and long-lasting that it can be called a dark night of the soul. If your main interest in life is health, you may quickly try to overcome the darkness. But if you are looking for meaning, character, and personal substance, you may discover that a dark night has many important gifts for you... It's time for a different way of imagining this common experience and, therefore, a different way of dealing with it."[42]

Gabriel was living in that dark night of the soul. He experienced this during the COVID-19 pandemic. The virus upended his world and ours. We can't be sure if such horrifying events are over. The next COVID may be lurking, waiting. Global warming and the potential cataclysmic changes that may happen could be even scarier. As I said earlier, we must reflect on this question: "Why this Storm of life? Why now?"

The next aspect is the action, What action has this tragedy called us to change as individuals and collectively as societies? Then we need to consider awareness, reflection, forgiveness, returning to love, and gratitude.

I asked Gabriel to get more comfortable on his couch. Our Zoom connection was good. I could see his face well. Everything was sharply in focus. He wore a tight-fitting black workout shirt that silhouetted his frame. The sliding glass door to his left appeared opaque as light shined tangentially over its surface.

"What came up this past week in your time of reflection?" I asked.

"I feel I'm going deeper," he said. His brow furrowed as he contemplated. "*The Remembrance* is doing something. It's working on my heart."

"It's helping the anxiety?" I asked.

"Yes, definitely, the anxiety is less," he said, nodding his head up and down. "The pain is almost gone now. Only when I really get anxious do I have the pain."

"Are you getting any revelations about your life?" I asked.

"Yes," he said. He nodded his head and scratched the side of his neck and ear. "I see now how the anger I have toward my father and the fear of being alone is connected. I keep asking for forgiveness."

"How is that going?" I asked.

"Somewhat better. I still have difficulty understanding and believing that I carry the light of the Creator inside my heart," he said.

"If you look into your heart, do you see the light?"

"No," he said. "But I don't see all badness anymore. The more I do *The Remembrance,* the better I feel about myself."

"It takes time," I said. "Often, it takes a few years of walking down the *Path of Love* to feel substantially better. You are making incredible progress. Let's move deeper. Why don't you get more comfortable?" I watched as he laid his head back and slumped down in a relaxed pose.

"Let's start with *The Remembrance,*" I said.

Once again, we started the healing session. We began repeating the sacred word he liked to use in *The Remembrance.* Together, we chimed the holy word. He let it flow deeply into his heart. I watched as his face softened. His arms relaxed. We carried on in that fashion as usual.

"Now, how are you feeling?" I asked. "Are any pictures or feelings in your heart?"

"No, my heart feels good. Quiet and calm," he said.

"I'd like to introduce a new concept to you in this session," I said

"Okay," he said quietly as he relaxed.

"I want you to keep your awareness in your heart region. Let your head drop down and put all of your focus and attention beneath your sternum, where your heart resides," I said.

I watched as he dropped his chin and head down.

"That's it. Look right into your heart region with your focus," I said. "How does your heart feel?"

He thought for a few minutes as he checked his heart. "It feels good. Soft and calm. I feel good. Very good," he said.

"Please keep your attention there," I said. Now, I want you to search your heart's emotions and think of something that you feel grateful for in your life. Think about all the things in life that you have, such as your health and a roof over your head, and everything you might be thankful to your Creator for.

"Okay," he said. We waited a few moments as he did this.

"Do you have anything you are grateful for?" I asked.

He was silent. I waited patiently. Slowly, he began speaking.

"Yes, I'm grateful." He let a moment pass as he collected his thoughts. "I'm grateful that I have my brother and that he is supporting me in this difficulty I'm going through," he said.

"Good. Anything else?" I asked. He then began relating several things for which he was grateful. He was thankful that he had a place to live, food, and enough money. He said he was grateful for his sisters, brothers, and mother.

"Okay, let yourself feel your heart again. How does your heart feel?" I asked.

He was quiet for a while as he searched within.

"Wow, my heart feels better. It seems more open. I feel calmer and more peaceful," he said excitedly.

"Yes," I said. "This is the power of gratitude." I related to him the teaching from the All-Merciful that says, "If you are grateful. I will increase you."[43]

"Yes, I can feel that," he said. "The gratitude is doing something to my heart. It feels more open, wider."

"Okay, keep your focus inside your heart," I said. "Let's go back to *The Remembrance*."

We returned to saying *The Remembrance* repeatedly. Gabriel's chest rose and fell with each repetition of the Name, and his body posture relaxed even more.

"Keep your focus on your heart," I said. "Keep all your awareness at the heart level. Now, I would like to see if you can thank your Creator for the anxiety, panic, and sense of paralysis that has overtaken you since you became ill."

I noticed a shudder move through his body.

"You want me to be thankful for all the bad stuff I've been going through?" he said. He opened his eyes and rolled them slightly. "That's hard to do."

"Yes, it is hard to do," I said, but looking for a blessing in our difficulties can be a big
step. I paused, then asked, "Can you see this?"

"Yes, in my mind, I hear what you are saying. But I don't know If I can be thankful for it.

That's a pretty heavy idea," he said.

He had opened his eyes, and was watching me now. I nodded my head.

"Yes, it is quite a leap. It is a giant leap of faith. It takes believing that your Creator loves you deeply. Like a parent, He is willing to let you touch the fire and be consumed by the fire of His love."

"Fire of His love?" he asked.

"Yes, when the All-Merciful wants to draw us closer to

Himself, he cooks us in the fire of His love. He allows difficulty and challenges to batter us like a storm. Things happen to us to burn away the veils that hide His love and light. He has used the disaster to wake you up. He is calling you to Himself. Just as He is calling all of humanity through great tragedies. He is calling us all to change, to embrace honesty, kindness, mercy, compassion, and all the good qualities that our hearts so desperately need," I said.

"I see," he said, knitting the muscles in his forehead. He was silent.

"When you are feeling the panic, when the fear and pain overtake your body, I would like to see if you can say *Thank You*. I want you to see if you can be grateful for your illness."

Gabriel raised both his arms and hands halfway up in a stopping motion. His eyes shifted.

"That's going to be hard, very hard," he said. He pursed his lips and shook his head a little bit. "I'm not sure I can do that."

"Yes, it is a very deep spiritual walk. It is a strong movement down the *Path of Love*. Being thankful for difficulties takes work." I told him that I had struggled with this concept over the thirty years I had been on the Sufi *Path of Love*. Only continual prayer and reflection enabled me to embrace and apply the idea. It was something I had to remind myself about continually. Even today, it's still a challenge to look past my pain to see the blessings. "But it can be done," I told him.

"First, I want you to reflect on this. Each evening, when you sit down to do *The Remembrance,* I want you to begin entertaining the idea that what happened to you was necessary. It was essential for you to change your life. Next, I want to see what it

Practicing Gratitude

feels like in your heart to say thank you and really mean it."

Gabriel thought about this for a second. "Okay, I'll try," he said.

The gift of being grateful is a powerful tool for opening and healing our hearts. Consider making it a part of your daily reflection and practice. Search your heart and your life. What makes you feel grateful? Every day, repeat the process of practicing gratitude. Soon, we will discuss developing a daily habit of heart connection. It will be a time when you remember the All-Loving, The All-Compassionate. Realize that you are still breathing. You are alive. But only our Creator knows what upheaval, wars, and plagues will come. Call to the Divine. Send out your calls of gratitude and wait to receive your increase. It will come. It is a promise from the All-Merciful, All-Loving.

He is the greatest of mothers. He loves you more than you love yourself.

Don't wait. It's time to move forward in your life.

Below, I've listed some simple ways to become more grateful.

PRACTICAL STEPS FOR PRACTICING GRATITUDE

1. During your time of reflection, list 10 things you are grateful for. Write them down. Don't do this superficially. Rack your brain to come up with things that touch you emotionally. For example, one of the key things I'm grateful for in my life is that I am blessed with an amazing wife who cares deeply

about me. All I must do is sit and think about her mind-blowing qualities, and, instantly, my heart becomes soft. I feel true gratitude. Next to being grateful about being led to the *Path of Love*, it's at the top of my list. Spend some quality time and come up with your list of ten things. Write this list down.

2. Next, tape this list to where you'll see it every morning when you prepare for your day's activities. The bathroom mirror is a great place to post it.

3. Each morning, pick one item from the list and spend 5 minutes thinking about it. If you've set up a time for morning reflection, let this be the time you feel your gratitude deeply in your heart.

4. The next morning, choose another item. Reflect again.

5. If you do this correctly, you'll soon find that feeling gratitude for the beautiful things in your life lifts your spirit and fills you with a sense of well-being.

9

GIVE YOURSELF HOPE AND MERCY

*Only when it's dark enough
can you see the stars.*
—MARTIN LUTHER KING, JR

"Give people hope. Without hope, no healing can happen." My spiritual guide shared this wisdom as I sat with him outside in my garage. Typical Michigan weather, with overcast skies and a persistent drizzle of moisture, had driven us from the patio to seek shelter in the garage. It was the summer of 1997. I was perched next to him, listening as people came to him with questions, and he counseled his spiritual followers who were journeying down the *Path of Love.*

Muhammad ar-Rifa'i was a physician of the heart—not a doctor in the usual sense, but something greater. He could steer troubled souls toward inner tranquility and healing. He was a Sufi Master, a guide of love. He was familiar with ancient knowledge of plant-based medicine, but his transmission of love was his real healing power.

He was in his early sixties when I first met him. He had chosen me to be one of the teachers who shares the *Path of Love* with whoever gravitated to my orbit. I had been on the path for a few years. Besides practicing traditional cardiology, I was also doing heart-based healing work. He encouraged me to sit with him to watch and listen as he helped people who were suffering. Their problems varied—physical, emotional, and spiritual. Sitting with and watching him enabled me to understand how he worked with people's hearts.

It was toward the end of a long day. He sat unimposingly in a lawn chair, smoking a tobacco water pipe. He wore a plain gray Jellaba, a traditional covering worn by Arabic men. It was one piece from head to toe, much like a woman's dress. Brown sandals strapped from behind the heel covered his feet. His face was oval, and a quick smile always adorned it.

"Always give people hope," he said, turning his face toward me to see if I was listening. "A doctor has always to give people hope. Without hope, no healing can happen."

I nodded, confirming that I understood what he was trying to convey. He smiled his infectious smile of love. Over the next twenty years of training with him, I watched how he lived and shared the message of hope and mercy with everyone who sought his counsel.

Hope is an essential ingredient for healing your anxious heart. Anxiety attacks, divorce, illness, or a horrific loss can lead a person to thrash about in a disturbing emotional wilderness. They feel lost and alone. They often clamor for *one good reason* to pull themselves out of bed each morning. I see them often in my cardiology practice. Patients whose lives are stalled, fearful of a heart attack brought on by chest pain and memories of a father or mother who suffered a massive coronary. Other times, it's a tachycardia that worries and befuddles them. Their heart pounds uncontrollably, producing sweaty palms, near fainting, and a feeling that the world might be slipping away. Much of my work is to prescribe the balm of hope. We do cardiac tests such as an ultrasound of the heart or a stress test to ensure nothing is seriously wrong with the heart. Often, these examinations yield normal results, and then I reassure them they don't have a serious heart illness. They are not going to pass away or become a cardiac cripple like their beloved relative.

Everyone needs hope. Hope is more than a feeling or thought. Hope is a choice. As we peer down the long, dark tunnel of life's difficulties and challenges we must choose to search for the light within the darkness. If we succumb to the darkness, we will only know despair. The key thing to remember is "You can be well." Countless people have utilized the technique of *The Remembrance*, and their hearts have found relief. Embrace hope. Cling to the idea that maybe, just maybe, your life can blossom once again after the storm.

Gabriel called again on a Saturday.

November skies were gloomy. The clouds were dense, silver-gray, and oppressive, like the mood he was in.

"I seem to be moving backward," he said. "I've been doing *The Remembrance* regularly, at least fifteen to thirty minutes a day. But I feel like I'm sinking beneath the waves."

His head was down. He slumped on the couch. I could see out his balcony window. Even though it was eleven o'clock in the morning, no sunlight penetrated the room. He was wearing a black Nike "Just Do It" T-shirt and gray sweatpants. The dark shadows of a beard framed his face. He hadn't shaved, and his hair sprang out in all directions.

"I don't know," he said. "It seemed like I was getting better. The chest pain is mostly gone; the feelings of anxiety had been getting better. Then out of nowhere, I'll suddenly feel anxious again. It's like there's a dam inside of me, and the water is mostly held back, and then every so often, a floodgate will open, and a tide of water will submerge me again. And I'm back into the panic and fear. I thought I'd be better by now."

I tried to reassure him. "Listen," I said, "don't focus on the negative. Look how far you've come. We started doing these sessions in April, and it's only November. That's just seven months. It took a lifetime of fear to accumulate inside of you. Years of torment at your father's hands have battered and bruised your psyche. You were in Italy working with that mentally ill girl for nearly a year. These pictures of suffering, anger, and resentment have been building and germinating. For years, they have strangled your innermost emotions and feelings. Shoved deep inside, they grew into a dense veil covering your heart. Now they are slowly working themselves out, and you've made tremendous progress."

I peered at him to see how he was reacting to my words. I could tell he had listened, but his posture hadn't changed. Something told me he wanted to break through his old ideas but was holding back.

"Can't you see the progress you've made?" I asked.

I continued watching him. I paused. He shifted on the couch

and drew his legs from the floor, stretching them sideways beside him. The angles of his mouth drifted downward in a morose appearance. He shrugged.

"Yeah, I can see I'm different," he said. "I am doing the reflection and *The Remembrance*. I never did that before."

"And you feel something now, don't you? In your heart?" I said. He nodded.

"Yes, I didn't realize it before, but I was mostly numb and angry. Angry without knowing why."

"You see, the process is working. Healing the heart is a slow process," I said. "That's why we call it *walking* the *Path of Love*. The healing that is shifting your whole personality is a journey. It's a transformative journey within your own heart toward inner peace. Like any difficult journey, it takes time. The road can be steep. Think about climbing a mountain. The path isn't straight. You go up, and you go down. You twist, and you turn. It's like I said, it's a dance through a storm. It seems like it has been a long time, but it's been a short time in the overall scheme of emotional development. I've worked with people who have struggled through twenty years of psychotherapy and have not made the progress you've made in seven short months. You are indeed moving at a breakneck speed."

"I just wish it was faster," he said. "I want my life back. I want the old me back—the happy guy who wasn't afraid or anxious." He paused, thinking.

I didn't say anything; I just nodded my head. The silence deepened.

"You're not saying anything," he said finally.

"No, I'm not," I said. "I want you to think about what you just said to me." I smiled and looked at him, cocking my head sideways.

He thought for a few moments. Slowly, a pensive look crawled across his face. "The old me?" he said, interpreting my silence.

"Yes, the old you," I said. "Did the old you serve you well?"

"No," he said sheepishly. I reminded him that the "old" him had been filled with anger. He was judgmental, not only of himself but of others. "When I look at you now, I see a different person. The rage has receded. A light has penetrated your face, and now it is softer. Do you feel that?"

"Yes, the anger is better," he said. "Things don't bother me like they used to." He pursed his lips and nodded his head up and down.

"The journey happens in its own time," I said. Often, we don't recognize we are changing, but the more we give ourselves mercy, the easier it becomes.

"What do you mean by giving myself mercy?" he asked.

I looked at him as he fidgeted on the couch.

"Giving mercy means that you go easy on yourself. You throw off self-recrimination and blame," I said. I reminded him that one of the emotional issues we had uncovered in his healing sessions was his fear that God wouldn't forgive him for not standing up to his father to stop the abuse.

"Do you remember that session?" I asked. I studied his face. He cocked his head to the side and scrunched his lips together in an agreement gesture.

"Yes, I've been focusing on this in my daily heart connection practice," he said.

"And have you been able to move past the feelings of blame

Give Yourself Hope and Mercy

so they don't bother you so much?" I asked.

"No, I haven't been able to get rid of those feelings completely," he said.

"Well, this is what I mean by giving mercy to yourself. It's being gentle with yourself. When we give mercy, we suspend judgment and offer ourselves compassion. When our minds want to plunge into endless loops that tell us we're a bad person or we are worthy of blame, we steer our thoughts in a different direction. We utilize *The Remembrance* and connect to our hearts to stop the mind games.

"Okay, let's see if we can uncover this as we move deeper and connect more fully to your heart," I said. I asked him to lie back on the couch and get comfortable. We started first with the relaxation exercises, then deep breathing, and finally, *The Remembrance*.

"Now, each time you say Ahhhh, I want you to let it move fully into your heart."

One of the keys to doing *The Remembrance* is to take the sound deeply into the heart. It's a skill that often feels foreign in the beginning, but over time, if utilized properly, the sound and vibration of the Divine Name will infuse the heart with tranquility and a sense of opening. Some people experience a *shudder* or a vibratory hum within their hearts. It's a physical experience, like when a person holds their breath for a long time and begins to feel like their chest is expanding or filling up. As a teacher of this technique, it's easy to discern how deeply a person is moving into their heart by listening to the quality of their *Remembrance*.

I listened to Gabriel doing *The Remembrance*. In the short

time we had been working together, a dramatic shift had occurred in his practice of *The Remembrance.* In the beginning, his words remained on the surface. It was like they were just words spoken with the tongue and mouth. You could hear them, but they remained lodged in the throat. They didn't penetrate further into his chest. His breath also didn't move deeply. It, too, was superficial. Now, everything was different. When Gabriel said Ahhh, the sound moved from the throat, flowed down into his chest, and then moved even further into his toes. It was a full-body experience of sound and breath. Just by listening to him, it was clear to me that he was going deeper. Also, he was fully relaxed. His head lay limply on the couch. His upper arms and chest were soft and tranquil. His lower arms were situated calmly near his thighs.

"Now, I want you to begin searching your heart," I said. "Ask your heart or your Creator, 'Why do I still feel guilt or blame myself?'" I waited while he did this. Together, we toned *The Remembrance* out loud. I watched his chest rise and fall with each deep breath. "Are you getting anything?"

"I don't see anything yet," he said.

I opened my own heart wider and began vocalizing *The Remembrance* louder.

It's common for a person to move deeper when working with an advanced healer than they can alone. Muhammad ar-Rifa'i writes in his book *Spiritual Medicine and Natural Remedies* that the ability of a healer to help another person depends on the depth of the healer's spiritual walking.[44] Think of a tennis coach. A coach who has been a professional and played at Wimbledon can better help a young tennis player reach higher levels of accomplishment. The same is true of healers. The advanced healer must have done their own spiritual walking, with untold hours of prayer and contemplation. In addition, the Divine must open the door for their success in doing the work.

We continued for three minutes. Slowly, I lowered the sound of my voice to just a whisper.

"Are you getting anything?" I asked.

"Yes, I see that it's about love. It's like I have a block from giving myself love. It's weird. It's like I feel I don't deserve to be loved." We paused for a moment as we both let this revelation sink inside.

"Keep your awareness in your heart," I said. We returned to *The Remembrance*. "Let's take it deeper." I lifted my voice, altering the timbre and giving it a rich, forceful sound. A person moving their heart down a journey toward inner peace can also do this. They can alter the musical quality of their *Remembrance*. Sometimes, a louder, stronger sound vibrates the heart and shakes the veils. Other times, a gentler, softer quality is needed. Today, I mostly kept the sound loud and strong. Like a musician, I sent wave after wave of *The Remembrance* to infuse Gabriel's heart with love.

"Now, what do you feel?" I asked him as I lowered my voice.

He lay very still on the couch. Not a muscle moved. His face was placid. Softly, I returned to *The Remembrance* as I carefully examined his face. Slowly, imperceptibly, a wave of awareness crested and rolled through his facial expression.

"I'm getting something," he said.

I continued with my soft tone.

"I see myself as a child. I'm maybe four years old. I had been very sick, and the family was worried that I might die. I had been losing weight and suffered from diarrhea. The water where we lived had a rancid smell and sometimes appeared brown. Everyone assumed it was unhealthy. We were poor, and everyone felt I shouldn't be drinking the water. My mother was uneducated, a country woman. Her sister, Hafeza, was college-educated and quite prosperous. She lived in a well-to-do neighborhood. My father envied her family. Hafeza and Mom had taken me to see a doctor because I needed frequent, costly visits to the doctor, and she suggested that she should take care of me. My father, who worried about the doctor's bills, had agreed.

"I see it all now. It's all coming to me," Gabriel said as he related the story.

"I think he should come with me," Hafeza had said to the adults in the room.

"I remember running to my mother and seeing the look on my father's face. I tried to hide behind her skirt. My father had made up his mind. He jerked me from my mother's embrace. My mother had yelled, No, she couldn't have me.

"But my father wouldn't listen. He slapped my mother, and she fell to the ground weeping. Hafeza took me kicking and screaming from my home. Over the next two years, I grew to like living with Hafeza. She had nice things and plenty of food. I filled out and grew strong. She dressed me in fashionable clothes and gave me new toys. Best of all, my father wasn't around. His screaming and outbursts of rage were absent. I wasn't afraid anymore. The

Give Yourself Hope and Mercy

beatings stopped, and I started to feel like Hafeza was my mom. And then, one day, it was all gone. My aunt had gone on a trip to Iraq. Because she didn't have my papers, I couldn't come. My father and mother showed up and took me home."

Gabriel became silent. I studied his face. Emotions were percolating beneath the surface. Slowly, a tear formed in the corner of his eye. He began again, retelling the story in real time.

"I felt that no one loved me. My father abandoned me, and then Hafeza let them take me back to the hell hole." Sobs began emanating from deep within his chest. His right hand came up and covered his face. Interestingly, he had repeated the same story that his sister, Sanaa, had shared with me.

"Let's go to *The Remembrance*," I said, beginning its cadence. Gabriel began to follow in a choked voice. We continued for a few minutes. Over time, his sobs subsided.

"Now, let's look deep. Let's journey into your heart," I said. "Ask your Creator to show you the wisdom of these events."

"The wisdom of these events?" Gabriel said incredulously.

"Yes, the journey to inner peace asks that we look past life's pain to see the wisdom. We have to look for the loving Divine hand moving beneath the waves of the storm."

I watched as a perturbed expression swept across his face, and his chest jerked slightly.

"I'm not sure I can do that," he said.

"I know it's difficult, but let's just see what happens," I said as I started with a verbal *Remembrance*. "Follow me." Sluggishly, he began. My voice was loud and rhythmic. His voice was halting, uneven and coarse. As we continued, his hesitancy lessened.

He surrendered to the rhythms of *The Remembrance* and let the music of our voices permeate his body and soul. After a time, I asked him to look into his heart.

"Feel your heart now. Ask your Creator to show you the wisdom of what happened to you," I said.

Gabriel became silent. In a delicate voice, I returned to *The Remembrance* and waited. Once again, I watched his facial expression for signs of an answer. The movement of his chest offered the first signs of acknowledgment. Gabriel inhaled deeply, held his breath, and exhaled in a long sigh. A look of knowing blossomed upon his face.

"Mercy. It's mercy, and it's hope and love. He said I was being taught the importance of showing mercy, giving hope, and grasping for love," he said.

"What do you mean?" I asked.

"My father was so mean—the anger, the beatings—it was like being trapped in a prison with no escape," he said. "But with my sisters and brothers, we created a life of hope. When he wasn't there, we collected together. All seven of us squished into one tiny room. We danced and we laughed. We created a life within the misery. It was like a Jekyll and Hyde existence. We learned how to overcome the pain and discovered the importance of being merciful to one another. And it gave us hope. Somehow, in the darkness, a light could shine."

He lay on the couch quietly. With each breath, the only sound in the room was the rhythmic rise and fall of his chest. I returned to softly singing *The Remembrance*—Ahhh, Ahhh, Ahhh—letting the soothing sounds wash over his being. I

Give Yourself Hope and Mercy

continued in this fashion for three or four minutes, letting this revelation sink into him.

"So, how does that impact you now?" I asked eventually. A thoughtful expression wafted across his face.

"I have hope, real hope. I've lived through the darkest times, but now it's behind me," he said softly. "I need to be gentle with the people who move through my life. I need to give hope to everyone." A broad smile flooded across his face. Slowly, he sat up.

"So, what are you feeling now?" I asked.

"I do have hope. I believe that my life will work and that all this pain has given me a new perspective on how to live my life. Over the last eight months, I have changed. *The Remembrance* is doing something to my heart. Most of the time, I feel better, and now I see why it was all necessary. Thank you."

"For what?" I asked.

"I see now that you were doing just what came forward in this session. You have been giving me hope. You've told me that things would get better. You were merciful to me. It's like you were showing me exactly what my heart needed." His smile grew bigger.

"Well, it hasn't been me," I said. "You've done the work. The All-Merciful, All-Loving brought you to me, and you've responded."

Giving oneself hope and being merciful to oneself cannot be underestimated. Without a flowing stream of hope, no one can sail forward. The heart's journey to inner peace is built on hope and mercy. When anxiety, panic, and loss enfeeble us, hope gives us the courage to keep going. It allows us to see the road through the dark nights that inflict our souls. Giving ourselves mercy lets us cauterize the inner recrimination that can hinder our progress. Everyone needs hope. All souls long for mercy.

10

THE REMEMBRANCE
THE KEY TO HEALING

Asleep or awake, writing or reading, whatever you do, you must never be without the Remembrance.

—RUMI

After nine months of suffering from panic, fear, and a sense of futility, Gabriel was finally obtaining relief. He had never been sick like this before. Previously, he had limited patience for people he deemed weak. He had always believed he could overcome any issue with mind over matter. Now, he saw that a person couldn't always think their way out of an illness. Mind over matter hadn't worked with his panic attacks. The searing pain in his chest hadn't responded to positive thinking. It wasn't always possible to push your way through an illness and come out safely on the other side. Inescapable hardship and pain could rack a person physically and emotionally to the point of breaking. Inner torment was a dark, stealthy opponent not easily conquered.

Gabriel had slowly been assimilating this revelation. It had caused him to worry that his easy, carefree life would never return. Although he tried to push down the doubts and disquieting feelings, they roamed just beneath the surface of his psyche. The slightest tremor of emotional difficulty could bring them pulsating forward. Yet, even though he wasn't well, he had to admit that something miraculous was happening.

The mighty storm that had tumbled through his life was transforming his attitudes and beliefs. His heart was softening, welling up with compassion and forgiveness. A calmness he had never possessed was growing inside of him. Like a plant that has pushed its way out of the soil, shoots of serenity were climbing within his emotional veneer. They were overtaking him at the oddest times.

One day, he took his Toyota Corolla in for a simple oil change and tire rotation. He had called ahead and scheduled the appointment. The clerk had said on the phone that they weren't that busy and the wait shouldn't be more than twenty or thirty minutes. He had arrived fifteen minutes ahead of schedule, and the facility appeared empty. After an hour and thirty minutes of waiting, he approached the desk. The clerk was absent. He could hear the chirping sounds of a video game coming from a back room.

"Hello," he said loudly. "He-lloooo," he said, nearly shouting. The red-faced clerk quickly came from the back room.

"My car?" Gabriel said.

"Oh, they didn't tell you?" he said.

"No," he said.

"The oil you need ran out last night and wasn't delivered this morning. They want you to reschedule."

Gabriel looked at the man. In the past, such events would

The Remembrance *the Key to Healing*

have caused him to rage at the clerk and slam the door as he stomped out. Now, he just nodded. "Okay, when can I reschedule?" The clerk informed him that the needed oil should be available the following day. Quietly, Gabriel rescheduled. He calmly left the office and drove home unaffected by this experience. The key to this new Gabriel was *The Remembrance.*

Throughout this book, I have been talking about *The Remembrance.* It is the essential way to clear the heart of the negative emotional pictures that create anxiety and depression and flood the heart with peace. Over the last twenty-five years, I have taught this technique to hundreds of people. People from many different cultures and faiths have utilized *The Remembrance.* I have worked with Catholic nuns, psychologists, psychiatrists, people of the Jewish faith, Muslims, Christians, Hindus, and people who are Native American— even people who lack faith. Everyone's experience of *The Remembrance* is different. For some people, the feelings of peace and contentment come immediately. Others have a more gradual response. Gabriel is a good example of a person who was a slow responder to *The Remembrance.* It took a few months of consistently sitting down, spending time in solitude, and repeating his sacred word before Gabriel began to experience real peace. But Gabriel persisted. He made the effort. He found a quiet time, sat down, and communed with the All-Loving each day, and, thankfully, in time, he came to feel the response from The All-Loving. It is a rare person who doesn't find some benefit from this practice.

The Remembrance has also helped people overcome real illnesses. I once had a forty-five-year-old man, Daniel, who called me on the phone because he was having an abnormal heart rhythm—Atrial Fibrillation. Atrial Fibrillation occurs when the heart's upper chambers beat out of sync with the lower pumping chambers. The upper chambers contract nearly five hundred times a minute, causing an irregular, chaotic rhythm. Daniel's heart had been out of rhythm for five months. Fatigue and shortness of breath hampered his ability to perform his daily activities. After suffering for a few months, he went to get a heart evaluation. His cardiologist had performed a battery of tests on him and could find nothing physically wrong with his heart. The medication that he was taking had slowed down his heart rate, but he still felt sluggish. Because of the persistent symptoms, he contacted me.

During our initial conversations, I discovered that Daniel had been going through a painful divorce. His wife of twenty years had left him for a younger man. Daniel was a high school teacher and was nearly ready to retire. The court would award his wife alimony and part of his teacher's pension. Shortly after the court hearing, Daniel's heart began fibrillating. During our first session together, we discovered that emotional fear was causing Daniel's Atrial Fibrillation. He possessed an overwhelming fear that no one would love him and that he wouldn't have the money he needed to retire.

Luckily, Daniel possessed an open and engaging mind. He had grown up a Christian but was willing to set aside his beliefs. He had no trouble utilizing the Arabic word for God, *Allah,* a powerful form of remembrance. He also committed to following the routine I outlined for him: awareness, reflection, and deep

The Remembrance *the Key to Healing*

practice of *The Remembrance*. In three short weeks, his Atrial Fibrillation lessened. As he confronted his fear over the next two months, his heart returned to a normal rhythm. Spontaneous conversion in this fashion without the use of powerful medications or having the heart shocked electrically back to normal is quite unusual. Daniel continued practicing *The Remembrance* and maintained a normal heart rhythm during the following months. Even a couple of years after our initial work, he was still utilizing *The Remembrance*, maintaining a normal heart rhythm and doing well.

Edward was another example of someone who achieved profound healing utilizing *The Remembrance*. Our paths first crossed when Edward came to a workshop I gave in the mid-1990s on living with a more open heart. I had been writing a monthly column in a metaphysical magazine in the Detroit area for a few years, sharing ideas about the connection between heart disease's physical and emotional aspects. During the workshop, I expounded on the various medical studies that documented the importance of treating emotional as well as physical heart illness. During the seminar, I introduced the participants to *The Remembrance* and guided them in a heart-focused meditation to connect deeper to their hearts. About twenty people had attended the workshop, but I hadn't noticed Edward. He hadn't asked any questions or responded to any of mine. He approached me after it had concluded.

Edward was in his early sixties, a somewhat reticent man of medium build with a black crew-cut streaked with gray. Large hazel-colored eyes dominated his face. They were sad eyes with bruised, puffy circles beneath them. From the corner of my eye, I saw him come forward as I placed my teaching notes into my briefcase.

"Hello," I said as he came near. "How did you like the workshop?"

He smiled, almost grinning, "It was wonderful," he said in a very soft, voice. "When I said the Ahhh, I could feel it in my chest. It's like something was opening."

"Glad you found it helpful," I said, nodding

"I wanted to ask you a question," he said shyly.

"Yes, sure," I said, now carefully taking him in. I couldn't miss those sad eyes. They dominated his face.

"Do you think your methods could help a serious illness?" he asked.

I lifted my eyes, pausing my packing up to let him continue.

He explained that he had a leaky heart valve. Two cardiologists had informed him that it was leaking so severely that his only option was open-heart surgery. He wanted to know if using *The Remembrance* and learning to live with a more open heart could improve such a condition. I explained to him that the work of Dr. Dean Ornish had shown that living with a more open heart could help improve blockages of the heart arteries. I explained that I didn't know if it could be effective in healing a seriously leaking heart valve.

"When heart valves leak, it's a mechanical condition, a structural malformation of the heart. I'm not sure if emotional healing could undo such a condition," I said. I also explained that most cardiologists wouldn't approve of using an unproven method for a possibly life-threatening heart condition.

The Remembrance *the Key to Healing*

Disappointment washed across his face. "Would you be willing to consider it?" he asked.

I thought for a moment. "Perhaps, but I would need to have more information. Why don't you make an appointment and see me in my office? We can discuss it further. But again, I can't make any guarantees." He turned quickly and walked away. I assumed I wouldn't see him again. However, two weeks later, I saw his name on my office schedule. He was listed as the last person of the day. My day flowed smoothly. It was an ordinary collection of traditional cardiology patients—heart failure, coronary artery disease, and heart rhythm problems. Finally, it was time to see Edward.

I knocked on his door and entered the room. He was perched on the examining table wearing a black sweater. The nurse had wrapped green paper around the lower half of his body. I greeted him, and we began the interview process. I discovered that he had been experiencing symptoms of congestive heart failure for over nine months. Heart failure is a serious medical condition in which the heart becomes unable to pump adequate blood to the body's tissues. A weakened heart muscle can cause it, from blocked heart arteries or faulty heart valves, as well as other precipitating events.

Two other cardiologists had examined Edward. They had performed a battery of tests to evaluate his heart's function. An electrocardiogram described a normal heart rhythm but with a thickening of his heart muscle called ventricular hypertrophy. A sound-wave examination of his heart, called an echocardiogram, demonstrated a profound leakage of a left-sided heart valve called the mitral valve. The mitral valve sits between the left atrium (the left-sided upper chamber) and the heart's main pumping chamber, the left ventricle. Normally, blood should only flow in one direction—from the left atrium to the left ventricle and then out through the aorta to the rest of the body. The mitral valve prevents blood from flowing backward from the left ventricle. In Edward's case, his mitral valve was not working properly. His valve was severely thickened, with prolapse (reverse movement) of one of the valve's leaflets. Blood was flowing torrentially in a backward direction. The echocardiogram report described an enlarged left atrium and significant elevation of his right-sided heart pressure. Heart pressure elevation in this manner would generally cause substantial breathlessness with physical activity.

Edward was suffering from a serious heart problem. His history confirmed the report's findings. Significant breathlessness restrained his walking. He could only walk about fifty feet without slowing down or stopping. Moving up steps was nearly impossible, and he even had difficulty lying back in bed. His legs were swollen and slightly bluish from the accumulated fluid. Listening to his heart confirmed the other cardiologist's physical assessment. A loud, rough sound of leakage of the mitral valve radiated across his chest and could even be heard in his back. After auscultating Edward's heart, I asked him to get dressed. I returned a few minutes later.

"So, what do you think?" he asked, looking at my face.

"Well, I agree with the other two cardiologists. You have a very severe heart valve leakage. You also have signs and symptoms of congestive heart failure," I said, pointing to his ankles.

The Remembrance *the Key to Healing*

He was wearing brown slip-on loafers, and obvious swelling was present. "Mitral valve surgery is the best medical option," I told him.

"But I don't want surgery," he said, pursing his lips and placing his hands on his hips.

I peered at him, gauging his mood and resolution. Very softly, I asked him why he was against surgery, or medications for that matter. Reviewing his chart, I noticed he wasn't even taking the water pill one of the other cardiologists had prescribed.

A look of sadness pushed upwards across his face.

"My sister died from mitral valve surgery two years ago," he said, pausing. A small tear leaked out the corner of one eye. He dabbed at it with the sleeve of his sweater. "I'm afraid I'll die if I undergo surgery," he said.

Silence dripped into the room. I waited for him to elaborate.

"We both caught Rheumatic Fever as children. We were poor, and my father didn't believe in doctors," he said then snorted. "But he believed in his whiskey."

The words from his last statement dropped to the floor. Once again, I paused. I now understood his fear of surgery. My heart went out to him.

"Most cardiologists would believe it to be malpractice not to recommend surgery," I said apologetically.

"Well, that's why I came to you," he said, his eyes flashing. "You're not most doctors. I've read your articles. You believe in the connection between the body, mind, and heart. I know that my mind is messed up. I've gone to some counselors, and they tell me I suffer from emotional trauma. Something inside of me tells me I can get well without surgery. So, will you help me?" As a cardiologist, I wanted to tell him I couldn't help him. I didn't know of any patients with such severe diseases who had been helped with non-traditional treatment. But I couldn't ignore those luminous eyes and his earnestness.

"Well, I'm willing to give it six weeks. We'll do healing sessions once per week for six weeks, and you have to agree to do all the homework," I said. "You have to be willing to practice *The Remembrance* every day," I looked at him seriously, and he nodded his head. "And you have to agree to take the water pill. Also, I will ask you to sign a disclaimer stating that you know this isn't considered acceptable medical treatment."

"Yes, I'll do that," Edward said.

"We will need to repeat the echocardiogram to have as a baseline," I said. "And most importantly, you have to agree that if you don't improve in six weeks, you'll be willing to have open-heart surgery." I eyed him closely. "Will you agree to surgery if it doesn't work?"

Edward sat calmly, his jaw moving back and forth as he contemplated things. "Yes," he said, nodding his head in agreement.

He left the examining room to go out and schedule the echocardiogram with the front clerk. Although I had agreed to work with Edward, I did so with trepidation. I had never crossed the line and ventured into the unexplored world of using *The Remembrance* to work with a potentially life-threatening condition. Of course, it had been effective in healing anxiety, depression, and non-serious heart rhythm conditions. This was different. Healing a structural anomaly of the heart seemed beyond

The Remembrance *the Key to Healing*

hope, but hope was the only thing I had to offer this man.

A week later, Edward returned for his first healing session. I had reviewed his echocardiogram, which confirmed severe leakage of his mitral valve. We exchanged pleasantries and reviewed his progress. He had been taking the water pill, and the swelling of his legs and ankles had slackened. He also said his breathlessness was mildly better, but he still couldn't walk up steps.

I examined Edward's heart. His heart murmur still boomed throughout his chest. His lungs were clear. The edema of his legs still pitted inward when I pressed with my thumb. I reiterated that we would try the healing work for six weeks, and if Edward didn't improve, he would need cardiac surgery. He agreed to my demands.

"Okay, let's start. I'm going to play some soft, relaxing music," I said, turning on a small portable CD player. I asked him to lay back and get comfortable on the examining table. I then performed the ritual of relaxation and heart focus. He had been open to using the Arabic word *Allah* as his form of *The Remembrance*. We chimed this together for a few minutes.

"Now, keep your focus on your heart region," I said. "Let yourself move deeper into your heart." He was silent, his face flat. "Repeat *The Remembrance* with me," I said. He responded in a low-toned murmur. We continued for a few minutes. Slowly, a pained expression fanned out across his face.

"What are you feeling?" I asked.

"I'm a little boy in a Catholic school in Northern Michigan. We're in class. Daisy, my friend, is being punished by one of the nuns. She had giggled in class when a boy named Robbie made a face when the nun turned her back. Daisy couldn't help it, and she laughed. The nun marched Daisy to the front of the room, and she made her hold out her hand's palm."

Edward's face now tightened into a look of horror.

"Now she's beating her hands with a metal rod. She keeps hitting her." As she said these words, Edward began sobbing. "Daisy is in pain. I want to tell the nun it wasn't her fault. Robbie made her laugh. But I'm too frightened. I'm just watching. I'm ashamed. I feel guilty. I should have done something. Why can't I do *something*?"

Edward's chest began heaving. I directed him back to *The Remembrance* and asked him to envision it going into the image. Over and over, we injected the soft timbre of *the Remembrance* into the negative emotional picture that filled Edward's heart. In time, his sobbing ceased. The shiver of his chest quieted. Finally, after his composure had returned, I asked him to sit up.

"Why did this picture come up?" he asked. "This terrible memory."

"I have the sense that somehow your feelings of guilt are related to your leaky heart valve. I don't know why," I said. "It's just the feeling that came to me as I connected to your heart."

I gave him his homework. I told him to do *The Remembrance* every day. I also asked him to reflect on his leaky valve and the feelings of guilt that had surfaced. Over the next six weeks, Edward and I worked together in heart-opening healing sessions. Each meeting was like a new exploration into Edward's inner emotional world. We discovered that guilt and shame were the driving emotions of his heart's psychic pain. As layer upon layer was unearthed and the subtle love of *The Remembrance*

The Remembrance *the Key to Healing*

penetrated his heart, his physical condition began to transform. Slowly but surely, the swelling of his ankles receded. The severe shortness of breath waned, and his ability to walk on flat ground and then up the stairs of his home improved.

I was astonished when I listened to his heart in our sixth session. His heart murmur, the violent cacophony of harsh sound, was gone. His chest was quiet.

He underwent another echocardiogram to confirm the improvement, and, amazingly, the mitral valve leakage had disappeared. His valves were still thickened, but they were more pliable. It was a miracle. As a cardiologist, I had never seen such a reversal of heart valve dysfunction. We continued to work together on monthly sessions for the next two years. During that time, his valve has remained free of leakage.

A third example of *The Remembrance*'s power is the story of a woman who read one of my books in my early years of my teaching this technique. She contacted me for help. She lived in New England and couldn't afford to travel to Michigan. I agreed to begin working with her over the phone.

I'll call her Alice to protect her identity. Alice was in her mid-forties. She was a believer, Catholic, but not currently active in the church. In a picture she sent me over the internet, I saw that she had shoulder-length, dark hair, deep-set eyes, and a broad nose.

On our first telephone session, I said to her, "Tell me a little of your story."

"Well, I started having anxiety attacks when I was a young girl of ten or eleven. They would be overwhelming. I had nightmares and a fear of going to sleep. The severe anxiety continued till I was an adult. When I was in my mid-twenties, I started going to counseling to try and figure out why I was having such anxiety and how to get rid of it."

"Did you have any idea what you were afraid of?" I asked.

"That's the strange part. I never knew what was causing the attacks. All I knew was that they mostly came at night. I'd wake up from a sound sleep and be frightened out of my mind. They've continued all these years, but now they're more intense. Sometimes, I wake up screaming and have an irrational fear of closets."

"Closets?" I asked.

"Yes, whenever I was alone or if I stepped into a closet, particularly a walk-in closet, the hairs on the back of my head would begin to stand up. Electric currents of nervousness would start to pulse into my arms and then my legs. My breathing would fluctuate and become shallow. If I stayed in the closet, I'd have a full anxiety attack."

"Did you ever discover what this was about?"

"No, never," she said.

"The psychotherapists didn't help?" I asked.

"No, they didn't. I went to multiple therapists and psychiatrists. I tried talk therapy and behavioral therapy and saw my priest. In all, I have had over twenty years of counseling and therapeutic methods. We never discovered what was causing the anxiety attacks. I even went to a hypnotist and a psychic, which also didn't help."

"Okay, so what brings you to me now?" I asked.

"Well, the panic attacks have been getting worse. I used to

have them four to five times yearly, but now they've increased. I'm having them nearly every week, and they're starting to affect my job. I've started getting anxious at work. I've also started developing some heart problems. I've been having chest pain and a racing heart. Sometimes, my heart will start racing at work, and I must stop working. I saw an article you had written in *Spirituality and Health* magazine and thought I should try something different," she said.

The first thing I did was recommend that she see her family physician about her chest pain and tachycardia. I wanted to be sure that she was physically safe. I wanted her to have a stress test, an echocardiogram, and a heart monitor. She agreed to do this.

"Do you ever sit down and do some reflection on your anxiety attacks?" I asked.

"Yes, sometimes I'll go out in nature, sit by a nearby lake, and think about things. Sometimes I feel a fullness in my chest area. Often, it brings on the anxiety," she said. "Do you think you can help me?"

"I don't know. Only the All-Merciful, All-Loving knows. I know that the work I offer is different from most ways of working. It's a method that works directly at the heart level. Do you think you're still interested?" I asked.

"Yes, I know something is happening to my heart, and I'm willing to try anything," she said.

We then started the deeper portion of our session, like the sessions I described with Gabriel. I taught her *The Remembrance*. She was Catholic but felt comfortable using the Aramaic Christian word for God. Aramaic is the ancient language believed to be used during the time of Jesus. It's the sacred word that I often ask Christians to use. The word is *Allahu*.

First, we started with the deep relaxation technique. I guided her to tense and relax the various muscles of her body. Next, we began with deeper breathing. Using *The Remembrance*, she directed her breath into her chest, deeper and deeper.

A profound shift occurred within just a few minutes of guiding Alice into her heart using *The Remembrance*. She began seeing pictures from her childhood. In the pictures, she was perhaps ten or eleven years old.

"I'm in a dark room. I think it's a large closet," she said. "Yes, it's an upstairs closet that led to our attic."

Her voice became stronger, raspy. Her breath surged.

"An older boy is with me. He's the next-door neighbor. He's maybe fourteen. I like him. I've had a crush on him for a long time," she said.

Now, her voice was staccato, shrill like a high piano key played repeatedly.

"He's making me take off my pants and panties. I'm trying to stop him, but he won't stop. Now he's on top of me. I'm asking him, 'Please don't do this,' but he won't quit," she said.

She started crying. The vivid memory of her sexual assault had come forward in the session. She had been too ashamed to tell anyone. Obviously, she had repressed the trauma deep into her subconscious and years of psychotherapy had not unearthed it.

We continued with the session. I asked her to return to *The Remembrance*.

"I'm afraid," she said. "I want him to stop." Her breathing

The Remembrance *the Key to Healing*

became even more rapid and forced. "Now, I'm screaming. I'm screaming. He's off me now. Nothing really happened. He tried, but nothing happened."

"It's okay. Don't focus on the pictures. You don't have to go there. Just return to *The Remembrance.* Say your sacred word for God, and take it into your heart," I said. "Let the sound wash the pictures."

She did as I suggested. She took deep breaths and let the Sacred Name flow into her chest. Over and over, we pursued the breathing and worked with the Name. In about ten minutes, the sadness and fear dissipated.

"How are you feeling now?" I asked her.

Her voice was calmer. Her rapid, shallow breathing had simmered.

"I'm doing fine now," she said. "That was amazing. I remember now. I recall that closet. I remember the boy and his weight upon me. I was so afraid, so ashamed. I couldn't tell anyone." She sighed deeply. "All these years, I've lived with the anxiety, the fear." Her voice was rapid and jerky. "I've always been frightened of dark places and closets, and I never knew why." Sadness and regret filled her voice. "All these years, all these years."

We talked for thirty more minutes. In a rapid-fire sequence, she went through all the ways that that horrific experience had altered her life. Little things, small fears and feelings of anxiousness, that she couldn't ever understand or explain. All the late-night awakenings of terror- now understood. Interestingly, it had taken heart trouble to get her to contact me. She had started developing a rapid heart rate called a Supraventricular

Tachycardia. She had been evaluated by a cardiologist a year earlier who had prescribed medication to control the heart rhythm. The medication worked most of the time but whenever she became extremely anxious the medication was ineffective. The racing of her heart had gotten to the point that she had started to feel like she might pass out. She was a teacher, and a couple of times at work, she had crumpled to the floor. The difficulty with her heart had pushed her to seek alternative treatment.

I asked her to begin doing *The Remembrance* every evening for fifteen to thirty minutes. I sent her an email with an audio file of a guided meditation, called the *Heart Connection Meditation*, for her to listen to each day.[45] I stressed the importance of making a deep heart connection through the use of *The Remembrance*, an essential skill for her life. She assured me she would listen to the audio-guided meditation and practice *The Remembrance*. I told her she could contact me at any time if she developed anxiety or had flashbacks from her traumatic event. We agreed to do another session in one month.

A month to the day, she called me for her second session.

"How are you doing?" I asked after she answered the phone.

"Fabulous," she said in a sunny voice. "I'm a new person, a completely changed human being."

She thanked me profusely and told me that her feelings of anxiety had vanished. She utilized the *Heart Connection Meditation* daily and did twenty minutes of *The Remembrance* every night. We moved deeper into her heart after a short discussion. Once again, the pictures of the sexual assault came forward. However, during this session, she didn't cry. Her voice

The Remembrance *the Key to Healing*

was calm. It was like she was watching someone else. In explicit detail, she described the sounds and smells of the closet. It was like the experience had lost its charge. The pain and agony of that horrible experience were muted. Its effect on her was gone.

Her anxiety and nighttime awakenings filled with inexplicable terror also vanished. We did several sessions together, but Alice was ninety-nine percent healed. The balm of *The Remembrance* had nourished and healed her heart.

Let's recap *The Remembrance.*

As I have discussed earlier, *The Remembrance* is a technique, a skill, an *intentional act* of bringing love into the heart through the form of a sacred sound. We use the Ahhh sound or a sacred Name for the Divine that carries the Ahhh phonetic. People sometimes ask, "What are we remembering?" We are *remembering who we are.* We are not the limited ego or psyche that most people envision when they think of themselves. We *are* the Divine light infused within our hearts. In *Remembrance*, we reconnect to that light and strip away the inner doubt, self-recrimination, and guilt that veils the full expression of that light. Pulling back the curtain shrouding our hearts is liberating and healing. Over the last twenty-five years, I have utilized this method to help hundreds of people clear their hearts of negative emotional issues that trouble them.

On a blustery Saturday, just nine months since he first began having his life disrupted by panic attacks, Gabriel and I met again online. He looked better than I had seen him before. His face was bright. He was smiling, not broadly, but he wasn't depressed. Sun was streaming in through the window off to his left. He sat on his green couch, not tense, just poised. We began with a few pleasantries. I discovered he had been doing his homework. Every morning, he would wake early and spend fifteen to thirty minutes, sometimes even an hour, reflecting on and utilizing *The Remembrance*. At night, before bed, he would return to reflection and *The Remembrance*. During the day, he tried his best to take his mind off his problems. He would bicycle to the beach most mornings, go for a run, and sit beside the water if it was nice.

"How have things been going?" I asked.

"Fairly well," he said, nodding a "yes." A small smile crept over his face.

Over the last month, we had done a couple more sessions, one every two weeks. We had talked about the need to be grateful for what happened to him, and he had been working on this.

"How has the work been going on the gratitude?" I asked.

"Well, you know that, initially, I was very resistant to the idea. Thinking that the horrific pain and the panic attacks could be good for me was difficult," he said.

"Yes," I said. "It is a big leap of faith."

"You've got that right," he said. "But over the last month, I've been reflecting and praying, and I've come to see that you have been right. My life was headed in the wrong direction. I've learned a lot from the illness."

I could see he was still thinking. His jaw went left and right like he was chewing on the thought. With each movement of the jaw, small shadows of light and dark spirited across his face.

"I didn't want to believe it. I mean, I almost refused to

The Remembrance *the Key to Healing*

believe it. When you first asked me to be thankful that these awful things were happening to me, I was angry," he said. "I was really angry."

"Yes, that's a common response," I said.

"I just wanted my life back," he said, and paused. Then he continued. "I still want my old life back. Of course, I know that my previous way of dealing with life wasn't good for me, but some of me still wants it back."

I explained that it was normal to want to return to the old way of doing things and of being. Our old lives are comfortable. They're like worn-out shoes that may not serve us anymore but contain fond memories. They have taken us places. We have lived and had fun in them. The outside preoccupation with life is tantalizing. It beckons with the illusion of happiness and fulfillment. But it is an illusion. The outer world can never truly satisfy us.

"Yes, I see that now," he said.

"It's important to hold onto *The Remembrance*. It's essential to continue down the *Path of Love*, to continue the journey toward inner peace," I said.

I watched as he agreed with me. He pursed his lips together in acknowledgment.

"Yes," he said. "Now, when I do *The Remembrance,* I feel such peace and contentment in my heart. It's indescribable. I never imagined sitting down, being silent, and just remembering the Divine could be so fulfilling, so satisfying."

I nodded in agreement.

"Sometimes, it is so beautiful. It's like your heart has taken you to another world you can't describe, but you feel so calm and tranquil. Your mind can't comprehend it."

I told him that I'd also had a similar experience. I've had glimpses of peace and serenity that were so profound, so overwhelmingly beautiful they defied all logical explanations. Words cannot describe it, making it even more difficult to discuss. My best explanation is sitting outside on a clear, dark, starry night, looking up at the horizon, then higher up into the heavens, and gazing, awestruck by the immensity that is our universe. As the heart expands, the wonder and beauty cannot be captured with words. All you can do is feel. You open your heart, and the feeling of mystery and majesty floods you. Your heart expands to fill with the experience. At that moment, you feel the connection. Your heart experiences a deep and totally real connection with the Creator. But no words can contain what you feel.

Indeed, the Sufis say that the mind cannot comprehend the wonder and majesty of the All-Merciful. The mind cannot contain God. Only the heart, the sincere heart lubricated with the delicate oil of much *Remembrance*, can contain and experience the Divine.

The Remembrance is the grease that softens and opens the heart. It peels away the layers of rust that have accumulated and stifled our hearts. It shakes the pictures, the negative movies that cloud us from the inner light. In time, *the Remembrance* dissolves these veils. They fly away, and we come to experience the Divine Light more and more.

Repetition is the mother of necessity. It is necessary to repeat *The Remembrance* over and over. Remember the analogy of the

The Remembrance *the Key to Healing*

river. If you want to purify your heart and clean it from negativity, it is essential to come to the river for washing. Dip the fabric of your heart into the river and wash it repeatedly. The more you sit quietly, reflect, and wash your heart, the more your heart will be healed. The dark grime of anger, envy, and jealousy will be lifted. You won't have to struggle and fight the negative emotions. In time, they will go.

Let me share with you a story about a young man whom I'll call Joseph. I worked with him many years ago. He came to me because he was deeply disturbed by runaway thoughts in his mind. He had been working as a computer programmer for a large corporation in the South for fifteen years.

Two years before he came to see me, his wife had passed away. She was in her early forties. He had shown me a photo of her standing at the beach. She was a beauty. Tall and slender, her hair was black, gleaming with an almost liquid quality. Her smile was wide, and looking at her eyes, you could see she was loving and full of life. Unfortunately, breast cancer claimed her at a young age.

"She could have lived," he said, crying in the office. "I could have saved her."

"How so?" I said.

Six months before her diagnosis, I had felt something in her breast. But I didn't say anything. My mother died of breast cancer, and I was so afraid she would die too. She was everything to me. Now, I can't stop thinking about it. These thoughts run through my head in an uncontrollable river of anguish. They won't stop. I've been to psychiatrists. I've taken countless pills.

"The medicine doesn't help?" I asked.

"No, it numbs me up. I'm like a walking zombie, but they don't stop the thoughts. 'You could have saved her. It's your fault.' They bombard me day and night. I can't escape them." He held his hands up to his head.

"What did the psychologist say?" I asked.

"She said I'm experiencing guilt. She says I should think positively. Get busy. She says it's not my fault. But my mind tells me that it is my fault. I could have saved her, but I didn't," he said.

During that time in the office, I practiced *The Remembrance* with him. I gave him homework like I gave Gabriel and the others. We found a sacred word for God that he felt comfortable using. I asked him to spend fifteen minutes each day in *Remembrance*. I directed him to do this very early in the morning before the sun came up, in the middle of the night, or just before bed. He agreed to use this skill as I outlined. He returned to me eight weeks later, a changed man.

He was bright, walking quickly with a lively step. A smile creased his face.

"When you first gave me this technique, I laughed inwardly. I didn't believe it could help. But because I was a total mess, I decided to try it. At first, nothing happened. I performed *The Remembrance* as you said, just using the Ahhh, the sigh. Amazingly, after about two weeks, something changed. I started to feel a little peace, a sliver of tranquility. But the runaway thoughts still troubled me."

He gestured excitedly with his hands. Next, he pursed his lips and began nodding.

The Remembrance *the Key to Healing*

"Then, one day, early in the morning, a strange thing happened. I began to get a sense of warmth inside my chest. In here," he said. His right hand came up and settled over his heart. "And that warmth began to spread all over my chest. So, I experimented. I switched to a sacred Name for God—one you suggested. Being a Christian, I utilized the Aramaic Name for God. And it was like a light switch was turned on inside my heart. A deeper feeling of warmth and contentment began to fill my chest every time I sat and did *The Remembrance.* About a week later, I was at work, focusing on an important project, and I suddenly realized that the runaway thoughts of guilt and blame were gone. They were no longer swirling uncontrollably in my head. The anguish, the anger, and self-loathing were ninety percent better."

I looked at Joseph. A broad smile blanketed his face. His eyes shone brightly.

"Thank you so much for sharing this beautiful technique with me. I can't begin to tell you how it's transformed my life," he said. He grabbed my hand and shook it wholeheartedly. "Thanks again."

"I've done nothing," I said.

It was true. I had done nothing. The oil of love from the constant repetition of *The Remembrance* loosened and extinguished his runaway thoughts, inner guilt, and judgments.

If your heart is anxious or you are suffering from anger or despair, I encourage you to begin the process of reflecting. You'll want to go deeper and deeper into your heart. You may find this challenging. In the beginning, you may find that the deep part of your heart seems distant. You focus but don't get anything. You may want the answers to a question that is troubling your heart, but as much as you try to find the answers, they do not come.

Understand that the opening of your heart is a process. It's like mastering tennis. Tennis is not the easiest sport to master. It takes hours and hours of practice to become good.

Don't be discouraged. Just sit quietly and focus on your heart. Do ten minutes of *The Remembrance.* Feel into the silence of your heart and then wait. If nothing comes, go back to *The Remembrance.* Say the Sacred word for God that resonates with you. Let it flow down into your heart. Over and over, repeat your Sacred Name or just use the Ahhh sound. Next, place your attention inside your heart. Sit and wait again. Listen very closely for a small, still voice, and trust the first thing that comes to your mind. You may not initially feel this inside your heart, but if you continue, it will come.

Stillness is the key. Get comfortable with the quiet expanse of your own heart. Return to *The Remembrance* again and again. You can do it softly or with a louder voice. Try to take the Ahhh down into your heart. Let it flow there with the breath. Let it swirl like water eddies in a river. Let *The Remembrance* flow over and over. Let it soothe and penetrate your heart. Persist until you begin to feel your heart starting to expand. With expansion comes tranquility.

Now, with your heart calm and expanded in this space, ask your question. In a very polite voice and a polite manner, ask Him the All-Knowing, All-Merciful the question about your life that has been turning around inside your mind. Then wait. Listen intently for that still, small voice, that knowing. It will be a whisper coming from deep inside your own heart and soul.

Occasionally, I have people who sit quietly, they do their *Remembrance,* but nothing comes forward. The key here is not to be discouraged. Remember the promise, "If you ask, I respond."[46] Hold on to this truth. Understand that truths and certainties do exist. They are the foundation of creation. If you're standing on Earth, you have gravity. It is a truth. If you drop something, it falls. It always falls toward the Earth. Water runs down a mountain. It doesn't run uphill. The sun rises in the east. It sets in the west. Again certainty. When the All-Merciful gives a promise, He keeps it.

The Remembrance, if done with attention and the intent to connect more deeply to your own heart, will lead to change. It will transform your fears, doubts, and uncertainties. Be patient. Hold on to the promise, the truths you have been given. Your life will get better.

Next, move deeper into silence. Crave the stillness. In the stillness of the night, when all else is asleep, you can find relief. You can return to your center, the heart. The more you practice connecting to your heart, the easier it will become. Soon, you will begin feeling real peace. You will begin experiencing the knowing that comes with a deep heart connection. This is *Inner Peace Now*. I write these things to give you hope.

Hope is the most magnificent truism of the heart. It gives us the strength to carry on in the face of extreme difficulty. Hold onto hope. Know that the All-Loving cares about you more than you care about yourself. The difficulties you are going through are His voice calling you. The disasters of your life are his silent call for you. He is asking you to return. Leave the fantasies of the outside and come to know the deep love that resides within your own heart. Remember, love is our greatest gift. Finally, understand that the All-Loving wants you to share it. Don't hold on to it just for yourself. He asks you to give. Give love to everyone you meet. Give it in a kind word. Give it in a smile. Walk softly on this Earth. Be gentle with the people you meet.

Soon, you will see this Remembrance flowing out of you. You will discover that it has enveloped your heart, uplifted it, and transformed you in ways you could have never imagined. Such is the mystery and wonder of the heart. Our hearts are The All-Loving's teaching vessel—the mother's womb. In time, the eye of your heart will open. You will find a peace that passes all understanding overtaking you.

I encourage you to make the journey. You will not be disappointed.

11

DEVELOP A DAILY HEART CONNECTION

*You'll never find peace of mind
until you listen to your heart.*
—GEORGE MICHAEL

The February sky was bright. It was a sunny warm day in the South. Gabriel had contacted me the night before, asking for a session. He agreed to meet in the morning, a Saturday.

We connected on Zoom. "Hi! How are you doing?" I asked him. He was again living with his sister. I could tell he was in the upstairs bedroom. A plum-colored painting of flowers adorned the white walls. He was sitting on a small, tan daybed.

"Okay now," he responded, "but earlier, I was having trouble," he said, concern creasing his face.

"Why's that?" I asked.

"I have been doing well for a couple of months. The pain is essentially gone. Occasionally, I'll have a few twinges, but it's dramatically better. I had a bad dream last night and woke up feeling scared and worried."

What was the dream about?" I asked.

"That's what's so funny," he said. "I don't even remember what the dream was about. I just woke up with a panicky feeling, that I couldn't shake. I went back to doing *The Remembrance*."

"Did that help?" I asked. His face brightened. He shifted on the couch, getting more comfortable.

"Yes," he said. "It made me feel better. But I was still afraid."

We discussed what had happened over the nine months since we had started working together. I reminded him how we had been making what I would call a journey into his deep heart, moving through the veils of pain and suffering that had accumulated during his lifetime. He was truly on his *Inner Peace Now* journey.

"Do you remember your first few sessions?" I asked.

"Yes," he said.

"Remember how our beginning sessions focused on the trouble you had in Italy with the girl who was suffering from mental illness? How you feared losing your mind and becoming like her? And then we moved deeper into the issues of self-worth caused by the beatings from your father?" I said.

I watched him shift on the daybed. He was wearing a blue T-shirt with some band's logo on the front.

"Yes, I remember that well," he said.

"And then we tracked the feelings of fear deeper, into the feelings of your sister Sarah who had developed mental illness and eventually died in the basement of your home. You felt guilty about not having done enough to help her with your father and that she was alone, kept locked away down in the basement?" I said. He nodded again, confirming that he remembered.

"We have been working on the idea that when you feel fear

or pain, you step back and examine yourself from a different perspective. These fears and pain are part of a book of your psyche that you can pick up and put on a shelf. And, as you're looking from afar, ask yourself, 'Where are these feelings coming from?' Next, try to see how they relate to your journey deeper into your heart. Do this with your rational mind. Continue examining them dispassionately, looking for the root cause. You're trying to discover what is triggering these feelings. Then you'll be able to see the trigger bringing up the feelings of fear and anxiety," I said.

"And as you examine it logically, you'll see you are not your sister. Your dad isn't here anymore abusing you. Your family is around you. You're not alone. You're not going to die alone. Then go to *The Remembrance* and begin strongly putting the sound into the pictures that have created these negative emotions. Continue over and over, letting *The Remembrance* wash your heart. If you do this, you'll feel comfort," I said.

I studied him closely. The calm expression on his face confirmed the positive impact of our earlier work and his progress moving through the journey to inner peace.

"Remember, we called this the process of heart connection. It is a skill for overcoming anxiety, fear, and other negative emotions. We discussed how a person learns to connect deeply to their heart. They use *The Remembrance* and bring love into the heart to nurture and heal their heart. The love begins to shake the veils and liberate the heart. It's a process that works seemingly magically."

"Yes," he said.

"Most importantly we talked about the storm, the damaging hurricane of emotional injury that started this journey."

"Yes, I know that everything happens for a reason," he said. "COVID-19 was the driving force for me to change."

"Yes," I reminded him. "So, what was the fear of the dream about?" I asked.

He drew his forehead up thinking. "I don't know. My sister has been ill. She's been having severe anxiety and feelings of depression. My brother and I have come here to help take care of the kids and help her. So, it has been stressful. Watching her suffering from anxiety makes it hard for me to cope."

"Let's, see if we can figure this out together," I said. "Why don't you lay back on the bed and we'll connect more deeply to your heart?" Gabriel pushed himself backward on the daybed. He slouched with his hands laying lightly to the side.

We started with the usual relaxation exercises. We did the deep heart breathing together. I asked him to begin contracting and relaxing the muscles of his body to release any tension. After we had done that for a few minutes, I asked him to bring all of this consciousness to his heart region, and focus deeply on his heart.

Next, we moved into *The Remembrance* together, slowly repeating the gentle cadence of breath and the sound of Ahhh, once more letting it flow into the heart. We repeated this for fifteen breaths.

"Now, I want you to ask yourself, your heart or your Creator—whatever you feel comfortable with—Why was I feeling anxious? What was the anxiety about?" I asked.

Gabriel was motionless. I could see that his head was tilted down, focusing on his heart region. His body was less tense; his arms were soft, and his shoulders relaxed.

"I'm not sure. I don't feel anything," he said.

Let's go back to *The Remembrance*. Together we began saying Ahhh, Ahhh, Ahhh, Ahhh. Over and over we used the warm feeling of breath to penetrate the heart. After a few moments, I asked him again.

"Do you feel anything?"

"Yes, it's like I'm starting to see something, feel something," he said. "I have done wrong things. I'm sad that I've done things I shouldn't have done. I'm sad about that."

"Do you feel like you can forgive yourself?" I asked.

"No," he said, "that's the issue. I don't know that I can forgive myself."

I told him to remember that God is the forgiver.

I reminded him that these feelings and images were repetitive. He had experienced this inability to forgive himself before. We discussed why similar feelings and images kept recurring. I explained that it's like peeling the layers of an onion. We have a session and identify an issue. Through the use of *The Remembrance*, we expose and release a portion of that memory, but the trauma is deep-seated. Quite often it takes many sessions and lengthy *Remembrances* to completely wash the area of the heart.

We spent further time in *The Remembrance*.

We discussed the man who had all the runaway thoughts. He couldn't stop his mind from thinking. He wanted mind control. I explained how *The Remembrance* organically helped curb the errant thoughts.

"You fear that you will be like your sister, Sarah, alone with no one to help you, but this is irrational. You are not her. You are not your sister. You are not alone. When you bring this awareness from the heart and begin to contemplate on it you will see that it has less power over you. Once you know the real picture of the fear and continually bring the light of love into your heart the negative pictures will go."

Finally, we finished the deeper movement into his heart, and I asked him to sit up.

Afterward, we began discussing why he was having trouble again.

"Tell me about your daily practice of heart connection," I said.

He smiled sheepishly and rolled his eyes up.

"So, you've slacked off? You haven't been doing it regularly?" I said.

"No, I've gotten away from it again," he said. "I'll do it for a few weeks and then once I start feeling better, I seem to drift away from it again."

"Not to worry. It can be like that," I said.

Developing a daily heart connection practice is like any skill; you must be persistent in your practice to see lasting results. As I have talked about earlier, to obtain the best results, it is important that you practice the skill either early in the morning or at night just before bed.

I had suggested to Gabriel that he get up thirty minutes before dawn. It has been my experience (recommended by my Sufi Guide) that the last third of the night is the optimum time for reflection and heart connection. Gabriel had followed my recommendation, but his efforts needed to be more consistent. Sometimes he would get up, and sometimes he wouldn't.

New habits take time to forge. The habits of our lives are like rocks. They can seem impossible to move. Training oneself to arise fifteen to thirty minutes before the first light of dawn is a challenging habit to instill. Perhaps you'll find it easier to Develop a Daily Heart Connection Practice at night before bed. Whichever way you want to do this, it is the first step.

STEP 1: SET ASIDE 10-30 MINUTES OF UNINTERRUPTED TIME TO CONNECT DEEPLY TO YOUR OWN HEART.

Performing the heart connection practice requires sitting quietly, becoming aware, and reflecting. Just like the healing sessions I have described in this book, you're going to want to become relaxed first. On my Facebook page, www.Facebook.HealYourAnxiousHeart.com, I've made available free guided medications to assist you in performing this practice. You can download them and listen to them at your leisure. I also have various video training courses at www.drkirklaman.com

To perform the connection process, you'll need to tell your family or significant others that you don't want to be disturbed for 15-40 minutes. You'll want to turn off the television, radio, and, most importantly, your cell phone. It would be best to leave your cell phone in another room so you aren't tempted to check it. You'll need a tranquil place to engage in this practice. It's important to be lying down or reclining in a chair in a totally relaxed position.

STEP 2: RELAX YOUR MUSCLES, FOCUS ON YOUR HEART REGION, AND BEGIN GUIDING YOUR BREATH WITH *THE REMEMBRANCE* INTO YOUR HEART.

You'll want to first start with some tensing and relaxing of your major muscle groups while engaging in some deep breathing to start the relaxation process. Next, focus on your heart, bringing all your awareness to the heart region. It's the area just to the left of your sternum (breast bone). Then, you'll begin doing *The Remembrance*. Be sure to choose a word you would like to use for this technique before you begin. Slowly, you'll want to bring *The Remembrance* deeply into your heart as you connect it to your breath through deep exhalation.

STEP 3: PERFORM *THE REMEMBRANCE* 100 TIMES. STOP AND FOCUS INTENTLY ON YOUR HEART. REFLECT DEEPLY ABOUT YOUR LIFE.

You'll want to do one hundred Ahhh breaths or use your other Sacred sound a hundred times. You can utilize a beaded necklace or set of prayer beads that contain one hundred beads, which allows you to take your mind off counting. You can also make such beads yourself from a craft store.

Develop a Daily Heart Connection

Breathe in through your nose, then as you exhale say, "AAhhhhhh." Let the sound go deeply into your heart. Pause for a couple of seconds as you feel the sound go into your body. Repeat until you have completed the full one hundred "Ahhhs." Next, keep your focus, your complete attention on the heart region. Now you can begin to reflect. Review your day. Remember the chapter on hope and mercy. How were your interactions with other people? Did you control your anger, your language? Where was the focus of your mind? Get clear about how you have been doing. Return again to *The Remembrance*. Complete another one hundred breaths. Once more let the sacred sound penetrate deeper and deeper into your being.

After completing the second set of one hundred Ahhhs, pause again. Now move to gratitude. Think about all the things you have to be grateful for in the world. Remember something in particular that you feel especially grateful about. Let this feeling or memory stir deep emotions within you. Let it warm your heart. Spend one to three minutes on this aspect of reflection. Return again to *The Remembrance*. Once more complete one hundred cycles of sacred breaths.

Now begin focusing on forgiveness. Search your heart to see if you harbor any feelings of guilt or anger with yourself. Find this place in your heart and bring the healing sound of remembrance to this area. You don't have to do anything special. Just let your breath and sound wash the area. If you feel inclined to call to your Creator you can ask for the All-Merciful's forgiveness and cleansing.

The next step of the Heart Connection Practice is to do one

or two final rounds of a hundred remembrances. This time, you'll want to seek guidance and knowledge about the events of your life.

STEP 4: DO *THE REMEMBRANCE* 100 TIMES. STOP, FOCUS ON YOUR HEART. ASK A QUESTION.

Here is where you begin to tap into the wisdom of your own heart. The heart connection process will allow you to plug into the stream of intelligence that is contained within the Divine light that lives inside of you. As you dance your way through the storms of life, the heart connection process, when combined with the daily practice of *The Remembrance*, will allow you to find the love contained within the difficulty.

Specifically, you'll want to direct your question to the Divine or your heart. Ask, "What are you trying to teach me?" "How is Your Love moving through or contained within this difficulty?" The more you focus on these two questions, the more profound your healing can be. If your heart can reach the place where you ask these questions and truly seek to know the answer, then you are indeed moving deeply into *Inner Peace Now*.

The final step of developing a Daily Heart Connection Practice is establishing this technique so it becomes a daily habit. Only by immersing yourself over and over into the healing waters of *The Remembrance* can your heart find solace. Like Gabriel, whose heart was shrouded by a lifetime of negative emotions, it may take time to peel away these troublesome veils.

STEP 5: ESTABLISH THE HABIT. DEVELOP A DAILY HEART CONNECTION PRACTICE.

The beauty of *The Remembrance* is that it is highly effective for most people, and years of negativity can often be stripped away in a few weeks or months. But you have to give it time. You have to put in the time to become well.

Establish the habit of waking up fifteen to thirty minutes early every morning and giving this time to yourself. In the beginning, it will seem challenging. Creating a new habit isn't an easy process. But if you persist and begin connecting over and over to your heart, in a short time, you will begin to find relief. The toll of the storms of life will lessen. Your heart will lighten. A profound peace will slowly penetrate your heart. Your life will be different. You will find the tranquility you desire.

12

RIDE THE WAVES

Dance with the waves, move with the sea. Let the rhythm of the water set your soul free.
— CHRISTY ANN MARTINE

Gabriel and I met again a month after his previous session. It was a late afternoon on a Sunday. It was a blustery day with varied clouds that caused light to dance through the windows at his sister's home. He lounged in the upstairs bedroom on the daybed with a gray comforter and large fluffy pillows packed behind him.

"How are things going?" I asked him. We were meeting again on Zoom. It had been eleven months since we had first started working together. He looked well. Heavily muscled. It was clear he was back to full exercise and workouts. His eyes were bright. No signs of depression or anxiety creased his face.

"They are going good," he said. "Better than I expected."

"How was dealing with your sister?" I asked. They had been visiting for a while.

"Well, it threw me at first. Being around someone who was severely anxious and prone to depression is hard," he said.

"Yes," I said, nodding in agreement.

"At first, I found myself getting anxious, but then I doubled my efforts at *The Remembrance*. I began working with my sister, trying to get her to become more regular with the practice."

I listened closely. Gabriel was sitting up straight, shoulders back. His emotional state appeared strong and balanced.

"Fortunately, it has worked. It took a while, but we've all been getting up to do the morning practice, and she's better. I'm stable, and it's helped her tremendously," he said.

"She was like me. She would do the practice, but when she began to feel better, she would slack off. I've been helping her establish a consistent habit of doing *The Remembrance*. I've encouraged her that doing the practice consistently is the way to improve. I've come today because I have some questions about her illness and her care."

We spent some time talking about his sister's treatment (with her permission of course). Throughout our discussion, I was pleased with the progress Gabriel had made. Eleven months of *The Remembrance* had been good to him. He understood the issues that had clouded his heart. He was making tremendous progress in moving deeper and clearing the emotional issues that troubled his psyche.

"Do you have any problems that you need help with today?" I asked. He paused for a moment, thinking.

"I thought that once my chest pain went away and the anxiety cleared that I would be completely well. I didn't think that I would continue having these flare-ups of anxiety."

At the close of his last session, I had encouraged him to

become regular in his daily heart connection practice. The journey to our deep heart, the journey to inner peace has its ups and downs. I sometimes liken it to a surfer riding the ocean's waves. The waves can be smooth or rough. Even after a person's heart has begun to open, the ups and downs of life can be challenging. It's important not to fight the waves and become submerged. It is better to ride the waves and go with them. Riding the waves helps us learn to put balance into our lives. We learn not to get depressed with the low points. We know that, like the waves, we'll eventually be climbing back up. We can enjoy the highs, and, when we swing the other way, cling to patience. Patience allows us to keep our feet firmly planted on the surfboard. We have to remind ourselves that everyone experiences these undulations in life. Rarely is life always down, and similarly, it's unusual for a person's life to be in the stratosphere continually.

"Let's look into that together," I said, motioning for him to lay back on the bed and get comfortable. We launched into the usual routine of our session work. After just a few minutes, he seemed relaxed and calm. We turned ourselves to the practice of *The Remembrance*—deep breaths into the chest and exhalations of Ahhh. With each breath, I guided him further and further toward a place of inner peace.

"How's that feel now?" I asked. Tranquility had smoothed its way across his face. His arms and hands were limp, and his legs stretched out and unmoving.

"I'm good. Very peaceful," he said.

"Like always, I want you to bring your consciousness down into the heart region. Let all your attention move into your heart.

Let the sounds from outside and all the activity in the room drop away. Let yourself be more and more relaxed. Let's do some more of *The Remembrance*," I said. Once more, we began toning the vibrational sound of Ahhh. Gabriel kept his eyes closed. I watched as his chest rose and fell in a rhythmic cadence.

"Let yourself go deeper and deeper. Visualize yourself walking down further into your heart. Allow yourself to move past any tightness or tension you might feel in your heart," I said. As I outlined earlier, guided meditations like Gabriel performed have been clinically shown to improve a person's sense of well-being. My own experience has shown that when combined with *The Remembrance* amazing openings into the psyche can occur.

"What are you feeling?" I asked.

His facial expression had shifted from calmness to one of searching. I could see his eyeballs moving back and forth behind his closed eyelids. It was almost like some form of REM half-sleep.

"I'm moving through a long tunnel. It's dark. The walls have a strange translucent quality, and I can see the faces of my family. They're like pictures on a television screen, yet three-dimensional."

I let him move deeper into his heart. I didn't speak. Rather, I murmured *The Remembrance* in gentle tones designed to massage his psyche. The sound of Ahhh softly swelled throughout the room like the ringing song from a Tibetan singing bowl.

"The faces, they're encouraging me. They're calling me to come," he said, his voice softening. "I'm moving forward to the light."

Ride the Waves

I watched his body closely. His arms and legs lay inert. All the tension was erased from his face. Rhythmically, his chest rose and fell with each pronouncement of Ahhh. I continued with *The Remembrance.* Gabriel said nothing. After a few moments, his eyelids fluttered and his brow crinkled as if trying to discern something in the distance. A look of awe now flashed across his countenance.

Suddenly, a loud AHHH exploded out of his mouth, catching me off guard. Quickly, he drew in a deep breath, and another AHHH, deep and long, passed from his chest and traveled through his body. At the end of the breath, his toes quivered slightly. With an open mouth, he sucked in another breath, and once more, a loud Ahhh rang through the room. I quickened the pace of my *Remembrance,* following his lead. On and on he went, loud and forceful—AHHH, AHHH, AHHH, AHHH. For the next four or five minutes, he continued in a thunderous remembrance of the Divine Name. The vibration rattled the walls, the air trembled, and his arms and legs shuddered. Eventually, the experience ebbed. His voice, now hoarse, grew softer. The quaking of his limbs subsided. Finally, he lay silent and still.

I lowered my voice but continued with *The Remembrance.* I held my heart open, feeling the pulsating movement of the Divine Name and the beating of my heart. Looking at Gabriel's face, I could see something was happening behind his closed eyes. It was like he was traveling, moving forward. I continued to let him be in his space. He was quiet, laying flaccidly, for perhaps five more minutes. Eventually, he stirred. His legs twitched and, suddenly, he blinked his eyes a couple of times then opened them fully. Slowly, he pushed himself up to a sitting position. Like being roused from a deep sleep, it took him a few seconds to catch his bearings.

"How are you?" I asked as I studied him closely. Something had happened. I could tell by the soft glow that emanated from his face.

"Beautiful, so beautiful," he said, in a faraway voice.

"What?" I asked, watching him closely.

He ran his left hand through his hair, pushing it out of his eyes. He blinked a few more times as a look of wonder eased its way across his face. "The beauty, the immense beauty," he said. "I can't describe it. The light was incredible, and the feeling of peace was so profound."

"What happened?" I asked.

"I was moving down a tunnel of light. The voices of my family were encouraging me. They kept saying, 'Keep walking, don't give up. You are the light.' And the closer I got to the light the more I began to feel peace. I knew that this light was the love of God, the All-Loving. I've never felt anything like it before. It was a peace and love that was so strong, so palpable. Like when you put your hand into a current of water, and it presses up against your hand. That's what it felt like. But It wasn't just on my hand. My whole body, my whole being was immersed in the peace. And I could feel the love surrounding me, moving inside of me. It was so beautiful," he said, his voice breaking.

Gabriel began to cry. Small droplets of tears rolled down his cheeks. "He loves me," he said, stuttering as he tried to choke back the tears. "I know now that God loves me. He wants me to be happy. He wants me to forgive myself." He lowered his head and sobbed softly. Embarrassed, he raised his hand to cover his face, but he continued to cry. His chest heaved up and down. He cried and cried and cried. I didn't stop him.

"I don't know why I'm crying," he finally said, trying to stifle the tears. "I've never experienced anything so beautiful. It was the most beautiful thing I have ever experienced."

"Not to worry, crying is a good thing. It is an opening of the heart and release of the veils." I related to him the story of my own deep heart opening that I shared at the beginning of this book. I had experienced hours of crying and then a tremendous feeling of oneness with the universe. It had been an amazing and transformative experience. Gabriel had now had a similar opening of his heart.

Sometimes, The All-Loving, The All-Merciful pulls back the curtain. He opens the door and allows a person to glimpse the indescribable peace that passes all understanding. The experience of such love and tranquility can be profound. It's almost as if the All-Loving picks us up by our feet and plunges us headfirst into the Divine living water of peace, love, and mercy. Stunned, we have no words to describe the experience. No mental framework exists to understand what is happening to us. All we know is that hearts tremble from the beauty. Souls shake with delight. And interestingly, it cannot truly be described. It is the unfathomable mystery of a Divine gift of love.

Many people who walk the *Path of Love* and make the *Inner Peace Now* journey are granted this experience. In the beginning, it may be small. Short glimpses of an intense serenity appear unexpectedly. It's like driving through an overwhelming thunderstorm of punishing rain and suddenly you crest a hill and the rain has vanished. You are greeted by bright sunshine and an unanticipated majestic rainbow. Then, five minutes later, you find yourself once again driving through the pouring rain.

Our heart's journey toward inner peace is a continual ebb and flow. Importantly, the more a person gravitates to *The Remembrance,* the more often the curtains are pulled back. In time, the heart is filled with greater and deeper love experiences. The brilliant Divine Light that lives inside of our hearts is revealed. Its soft, sweet, maternal embrace nurtures us. Eventually, any day without the deep heart connection of *The Remembrance* seems sad and empty. The traveler must continue to ride the waves—savoring the high points when The All-Loving gifts us, and asking for patience in the difficult times.

As part of my effort to help people in this work, I offer online help, audio programs, and video trainings to guide people in the process of deeper heart connection. I also offer webinars that can be accessed through my website—www.drkirklaman.com.

Over the next three months, Gabriel didn't ask for sessions. The amazing experience of the last session had changed him. He continued to come to the weekly *Remembrance* meetings and do the practices alone. I spoke with him on the phone one Sunday just to catch up with him. He shared with me some of what had been happening in his life.

"I've been doing well," he said. "The last session healed something within my heart. The pain and overwhelming anxiety have evaporated. I still get anxious, but it's like it's on the outside, running along the surface of my body. It's not traveling into my heart. Now, I'm not saying I don't have trouble. Work is still demanding and often stressful, but I don't let it bother me like before. Indeed, things are different.

"I've been doing some soul searching. I might want to go to college to pick up a skill or a trade. John and I have even begun talking about starting our own business. Even the anger I feel for my father has lessened. Of course, I can't say that I completely forgive him for everything he's done, but things are shifting."

Gabriel went on to say that he had talked with his mother on a video visit, and she had encouraged him to talk to his father and to try to forgive him. She shared some of Gabriel's father's history with him. He had grown up in an isolated and backward village in the south of Morocco. She related that the early years of his life had been one of fear and pain. She described the beatings that *his* father had inflicted upon him when he was a child and even a teenager. He too had grown up only knowing pain and feelings of worthlessness at the hand of his father.

She tried to tell me my father's actions, the way he terrorized all of us kids and my mother, weren't his fault. He didn't know anything different.

"I told her that wasn't an excuse," Gabriel said, a stern look flashing across his face.

"What did she say?" I asked.

"She agreed, but she wanted me to try to understand him and show him compassion. I looked at her frail, spent body. Her health has been beaten out of her with all the years of his abuse.

Just looking at her makes my heart fill with anger." He smiled slyly. "I don't know how many years of sessions it will take to let go of that anger."

I chuckled. "At least you realize that it's possible to change, to let go of the negative emotions that have inflicted your psyche and tormented your heart," I said. "Remember, we have only been working together for just a little over a year."

"Yes, it's incredible that I've come this far in such a short span. At times, I don't even recognize the old me."

"Yes, your sisters have mentioned that you seem completely different. They are most amazed at the change in your anger and how you approach life." I said. I'd had a video phone call on WhatsApp with his sister Aisha. She and her husband were living in North Carolina. Recently, the six brothers and sisters had gone on a five-day trip to the Smokey Mountains. They had rented a condo out in the woods. Being in close quarters with three kids and six adults had enabled them to experience the new Gabriel.

"I was astonished," Aisha told me. She was a well-composed woman in her mid-forties with shoulder-length black hair. Slightly overweight, she possessed large, beautiful eyes. She talked with me while lounging on a sofa in her living room. Her daughter of six played with some dolls at her feet. "Gabriel is so calm now. The old Gabriel was filled with anger. It showed in his face and how he dealt with people. The slightest thing could send him into a raging fit of anger. He'd be angry for days, stomping about the room, putting everyone on edge. Now, everything has changed. His face is softer, and even his voice is more tender toward people."

Ride the Waves

I related the comments that she had shared with me to Gabriel.

"Yes," Gabriel said. "That's true. It's the strangest thing. Over this year, I've noticed that my heart has shifted. It's hard to put into words, but Aisha is right. I haven't made any effort to treat people differently, but now I see them in a different light. The judgment I used to carry has faded. Oh, it's still there. People can quickly get under my skin, but it doesn't affect me in the same way. It's muted. Like a dimmer switch has been activated inside my psyche, and the strength of my judgment has been ratcheted down. I feel more peaceful as I go through my day."

I studied him closely as he sat perched on the bed. He *was* comfortable and relaxed. The scowl that had lined his face when we first started our sessions, the scowl that pointed his countenance into an exclamation mark of anger, was gone. Almost to illustrate the transformation, a gentle smile slowly wafted across his face.

As we concluded our session that day, I didn't know when we would work together again, but I was confident in his ability to deal with life's challenges. Gabriel was indeed utilizing the skills to create *Inner Peace Now*. He had learned the tools of self-awareness, reflection, and *The Remembrance* that would support him on his travels. The eye of his heart had opened, and he was engaging his world with a new perspective. The *Path of Love* had transformed him. His life would never be the same.

Oh, my readers, I hope you have learned from Gabriel's story. It is all true.

Don't wait for the storms of life to pull you under the waves.

Take your chance and begin walking deeper into your heart. Make your own journey toward inner peace. You won't be disappointed.

As my great teacher and guide has written, "There is no life like this life."

The journey into your heart is the only way to find the inner peace you desire.

13

WHERE TO GO FROM HERE

The present is the ever moving shadow that divides yesterday from tomorrow. In that, lies hope.
—FRANK LLOYD WRIGHT

Every person who desires to connect to the Divine is successful. A heart that longs to return to its source makes the journey and returns. "Seek and you shall find,"[47] is a promise. What you find when you read the sacred books is that the All-Merciful wants us to return to Him. He is longing for our return.

It is a loving longing. His desire is for us to be swept up in the peace, love, mercy, and joy that are our birthright. Yes, it seems hard to believe, but the disasters of life can be seen as his loving call. They are like a parent's reminder to their child: Where is your focus? Where is your heart?

Gabriel's experiences of deep healing sessions opened a vital secret for his moving further down the road to *Inner Peace Now*. If you want to go deeper into the peace, you must let yourself be taken over by *The Remembrance*.

What do I mean by this?

Inner Peace Now is based on the deep remembrance of the

Divine. This remembrance needs to occupy more and more of your thoughts and actions. It's important to allow *The Remembrance* to begin profoundly penetrating your heart. *The Remembrance* is organic. It's a natural experience for our psyches. It has been programmed into us at birth by our Creator. It is part of our DNA, as much as hair or eye color. Your heart wants to connect to this lifestream.

Doing *The Remembrance* is not just a repetition of breath and a sound. Doing *The Remembrance* is often a full-body experience. The combination of breath and sound indescribably reverberates inside us, affecting form and function. The Sufis say that *The Remembrance i*s the very foundation of life. Like a primordial wind that can sweep you up and engulf you, like being inside your mother's womb. Being overtaken by *The Remembrance* can be a life-altering experience.

All of us have had the feeling when our whole being seemed overtaken by a powerful event. Falling in love, for example, can take over your whole life—body, mind, and soul. When you fall in love, the excitement and newness can stimulate all of your senses. You feel completely awake and alive. Everything in life jumps out at you. The smells are sweeter. The flowers shine brighter. Your outlook on life is happier—full of hope and wonder.

Other things in our lives can overtake us. Perhaps you've had a time when you heard a song you particularly liked. You listened to it over and over. Soon the song seemed to take control of your mind. It won't leave you. You hear it playing inside your head when you're working, walking, and you sometimes wake up from sleep with it swirling around in your head.

Where to Go from Here

If you want to move deeper, further down your journey to *Inner Peace*, you need to deepen your connection to the love that lives inside of you to the point that it overtakes your life, just like that song. *The Remembrance* can do this. It can produce a profound change in a person's life.

Many people have limited ideas about *The Remembrance*. They see it as some religious indoctrination. Don't get caught up in such ideas. As I've said before, the light of your Creator lives inside your heart. Every human being carries this light. The light doesn't carry a religious creed or doctrine. *The Remembrance* is a method for peeling away the veils that shroud this glorious light. Discovering your inner Divine light is your birthright. It's built into your makeup, your DNA. If you don't feel comfortable with a Sacred Name for the Creator you can use the sound Ahhh, the natural, and organic sound that people in every culture make for true relaxation and inner tranquility.

The key is to find a Name or sound that works for you and to put it into practice. Consider developing your own daily heart connection practice.

If you want to heal the negative emotions that are clouding your life and overcome fear, anxiety, and other inner aches, embracing *The Remembrance* is the key. In the twenty years that I have been utilizing these heart-healing methods, I have been astonished by the results. I hope you can have a similar experience of deep heart healing.

Hopefully, from reading this book you have tasted some of the deep love that emanates from the All-Loving's call for you. I have tried in my feeble way to share a small drop of the love that is possible if you heed His call. The *Path of Love* awaits you. The door is open. If what you have read resonates within your heart, don't delay. Surge forward. Embrace *The Remembrance* with your whole heart. Plunge into the ocean that is its symphony. Let its sound, its music, vibrate every cell of your body. It truly is the Music of the Soul.

If you want to know more, go to my Facebook site: www.Facebook.com/HealYourAnxiousHeart.com. On that site, you'll find deeper teachings, audios, and videos with more information about transforming your heart. You can also go to my website: www.drkirklaman.com. I have additional books, audio, and video programs to help you heal your heart.

If Sufism, the real *Path of Love*, interests you, then go to www.facebook.com/SufiHeartAtlanta/. Learn more about the *Path of Love*. Sign up for our messages if you are so inclined.

My first teacher wrote: "Everything is in the way of the Love."[48] By this, he meant that we may see life as difficult. We may be swept up in challenges that stretch us to the breaking point. But the trials of life are not punishment; they are the Divine's call of love. A mysterious love is working its way through your life. It wears many clothes and appears to us in many different faces. Sometimes the faces appear harsh or angry. Importantly, beneath the harshness shines the light of love. My prayer for you is that you come to know the inescapable, transformational love that oscillates through every aspect of our glorious, created universe.

May God Bless You.

AFTERWORD

Five years have passed since I first began working with Gabriel Aziz. I have kept in close contact with him. In 2024, his mother passed away. Hadya had been Gabriel's rock of support and love. I was concerned about his significant loss and wondered if he would still be able to maintain the inner peace that *The Remembrance* had fostered in his life. Thankfully, his emotional and mental health has been sustained. Of course, life has its problems, and Gabriel, like all of us, must navigate the ups and downs. Importantly, his success can encourage readers of this book. If you commit to the transformational technique of *The Remembrance,* it can help you to weather all the storms of life.

APPENDIX

HOW TO PRACTICE
THE REMEMBRANCE

1. **Set the Stage**: Set aside 10-40 minutes to utilize this practice. Make sure you have no distractions. Turn off the cell phone, TV, or other devices. Tell your family members (if possible) that you need some time alone to do this work. Obtain a set of Remembrance beads. It can be a necklace or beads you have strung yourself. Amazon has a wide assortment. Just put the words "prayer beads" in the search line. There should be one hundred beads on the strand. You will utilize the beads for counting. This allows your mind to focus on your heart and not keep track of how many times you have done the technique. The beads should have some slack in them to allow you to move them along.

    Decide what word you will utilize as your form of *The Remembrance*. You can use the sound Ahhh. It's the universal sound of relaxation. If you're more spiritually inclined, you can use the Aramaic word for the Creator, *Allahu*. Christians who live in the Middle East and Arabic speakers will generally use the word *Allah*. Just be comfortable with whatever Ahh sound you prefer to utilize.

2. **Get Comfortable**: Ideally, you'll want to be lying down or propped up in bed. Be sure you are in a very comfortable reclining position.

3. **Start First with Relaxation:** After you have found your comfortable position, close your eyes and take a big breath in through your nose with a closed mouth. Fill your entire lungs. Next, exhale with your mouth open. Forcefully expel the air in a two-part exhalation. Say, "Hunh, Hunh." Feel this exhalation throughout your chest and all the way down to your toes. Repeat these relaxing breaths two more times for a total of three breaths.

4. **Bring Your Focus to Your Heart:** Now, keeping your eyes closed, place your focus, your attention in the heart region. The heart region is the area just to the left of your lower sternum. As you do this, you'll want to drop your head down. Imagine you are looking into your heart. Keep your awareness in this area.

5. **Say Ahhh**: Now you are ready to bring *The Remembrance* into your heart. Keep your remembrance beads in your hand. Start by inhaling deeply through your nose in one long inhalation. Once again, fill your lungs completely with air. On the exhalation, say the word you wish to use and let this sound move down into your heart region. Remember to keep your focus in your heart. Let the sound penetrate your heart. Keep your eyes closed, and move one bead forward.

    Continue saying Ahhh until you have gone all the way around the beads. At this point, you should have completed one hundred Ahhhs. Hopefully, at this point, you are fully relaxed.

Appendix: How to Practice The Remembrance

6. **Feel Your Heart:** Now, with your awareness remaining in your heart, be silent. Listen intently to your heart. Try to get a sense of how your emotional or spiritual heart feels. Is your heart calm? Does it feel tight or constricted? Is stress or anxiety clouding your heart? Be okay with whatever you feel. Don't judge it or do anything about it. Just be aware of what is happening inside at your heart level.

    Awareness of your heart may be a new experience for you. Allow yourself to be comfortable with whatever is happening inside your heart. You may see pictures of painful experiences that have troubled you before.

    If you do feel constriction, pain, or anxiety, know that you can stop this exercise at any moment. But if you don't feel overwhelmed, go back to step five. Keep your focus on the heart region and return to saying Ahhh. Only now, direct your Ahhh into the area of your heart that feels constricted or contains negative pictures. See if you can locate the exact area of constriction and send the Ahhhh, like a laser beam, into this area. Notice what happens to your heart. Does the constriction lessen? Do the pictures become less intense?

7. **Return to** *The Remembrance*: After you have assessed your heart again or sent the Ahhh into the troublesome areas, return to another round of one hundred Ahhhs. Keep yourself relaxed and calm. Repeat steps five and six again. Once more notice how your heart feels. Try not to do anything with the pictures or feelings. Let the Ahhh do its work.

8. **Ask Your Heart a Question**: After you have done three hundred Ahhhs and your heart feels calmer, now is the time to reflect on your life. It's also time to ask your heart questions. You can direct these questions to your Creator or to the wisdom of your own heart. Again, keep your awareness and focus deeply within your heart area. Next, ask a question about anything that is troubling your life.

   A good question to ask is: "What is the wisdom of what is happening to me with this problem?" Remember, we are trying to see deeply with the eye of the heart, looking past the difficulty to see the hand of the Divine's plan for us.

   Remain very still and calm. Wait for the answer. It's important to trust the first message you get. Often it will come as a thought. In time, you'll feel it in the heart region. The more you practice this technique, the more comfortable you will be with the reliability of the wisdom you receive. If you don't get any answers, don't be discouraged. It's not always easy to trust this form of meditation. It is more important to allow calmness and peace to enter your heart.

9. **Return to *The Remembrance***: Now, return to another round of *The Remembrance*. Repeat steps five and six. It's best to utilize this technique for at least fifteen minutes, but it can be helpful to do it for longer periods.

10. **Bring in Loving Feelings**: An additional technique for opening the heart is to bring a strong, loving feeling into your heart. Think of a feeling or memory that makes you

Appendix: How to Practice The Remembrance

feel love. Perhaps it's a memory of your mother, father, or other significant loved one. It could be your dog. Whatever gives you a warm feeling, bring this inside your chest as you say Ahhh. Notice what happens to the feeling of your heart. Does your heart open? Do you feel a softness inside your heart? Again, try not to manipulate this feeling. Just be comfortable with the sense of peace that fills your heart.

11. **Practice *The Remembrance* Daily**: The key to using this technique is to keep doing it. People often use this method when troubled or their heart feels pained. Yet, the best benefit is to flood your heart daily with the All-Merciful's love. If you utilize this technique even when life is going well, you'll soon derive even greater benefits.

ENDNOTES

1. 1 Thessalonians 5:17 (RSV)
2. Rachel Hollis, Didn't See That Coming. (Harper Large Print, 2020), p 3.
3. Civilla D. Martin. His Eye is On The Sparrow. 1905.
4. Muhammad ar-Rifa'i. Sufi Master. Lecture 2017.
5. M. Scott Peck, M.D. The Road Less Traveled. (Simon and Shuster. 1978), p 15.
6. Antoine de Saint Exupery. The Little Prince. (Harcourt. 1943), p 70.
7. Monica Gianni, Francesco Dentail, Anna Maria Grandi, Glen Summer, Rajesh Hiralal, Eva Lonn. Apical Ballooning Syndrome or Takotsubo Cardiomyopathy: A Systemic Review. Volume 27, Issue 13. July 2006. P1`523-1529.
8. Rachael Lampert. Emotion and sudden cardiac death. Expert Review of Cardiovascular Therapy. Volume 7, 2009, p 723-725.
9. Jalalu'ddin Rumi. The Mathnawi of Jalalu'ddin Rumi. Konya Metropolitan Municipality, 2004
10. Muhammad al-Jamal. Music of the Soul. From a Hadith Qudsi.
11. Malcolm Gladwell. Outliers. (Little, Brown, and Company 2008), p 35.
12. Mordehal Heiblum. Nature: February 26. 1998 Vol. 391, pp 871-874.
13. www.drwaynedyer.com/blog/manifest-with-spirit/
14. Waechter, Randall. (2004). Manipulation of the Electromagnetic Spectrum via Fields Projected from Human Hands. Subtle Energies and Energy Medicine. 13: 233.

15 Doc Childre. Howard Martin, Donna Beach. The HeartMath Solution. (HarperOne, 2000).

16 Missing Reference

17 Personal reflection of Shaykh Muhammad ar-Rifa'i teaching.

18 Breedvelt JJF, Am1.anvermez Y, Harrer M, et al. The effects of meditations, yoga, and mindfulness on depression, anxiety, and stress in tertiary education students: a meta-analysis. Frontiers in Psychiatry. 2019. 10:193.

19 Muhammad al-Ninowy. The Book of Love. (2020) p 5.

20 Chapter 3, Understanding the Impact of Trauma. Available from: https://www.ncbi.nlm.nih.gov/books/NBK207191/

21 Thomas Moore, Dark Nights of the Soul. (Gotham Books, 2004), introduction.

22 Muhammad al-Ninowy. The Book of Love. (2020) p 5.

23 Missing Reference

24 Doc Childre, Howard Martin, Donna Beach. The HeartMath Solution. (HarperOne, 2000).

25 Bernie Siegel, Love, Medicine, and Miracles. (HarperCollins Publishers, 1988).

26 Paul Pearsall, Ph.D. The Heart's Code. (Harmony Publishers, 1999)

27 Muhammad al-Jamal. He Who Knows Himself, Knows His Lord. (Sidi Muhammad Press, 2007).

28 Dean Ornish, M.D. Program for Reversing Heart Disease. (Ivy Books, 1995).

29 Mathew 7:7 (RSV)

30 Quran, 21:37

Endnotes

31 James Clear. Atomic Habits. (Avery, 2018) p 6-7.

32 Robert Enright. Eight Keys to Forgiveness. (W.W. Norton & Company, 2015), p 1.

33 Waltman, M.A., Russell, D.C., Coyle, C.T., Enright, R.D, Holter, A.A.C, & Swoboda, C . Dm, The effects of a forgiveness intervention on patients with coronary artery disease. Psychology and Health, p 24.

34 Muhammad ar-Rifa'i. Music of the Soul. (Sidi Muhammad Press) p 148.

35 Missing Reference

36 Missing Reference

37 Quran, 14:7

38 Muhammad al-Jamal. Music of the Soul (Sidi Muhammad Press, 2007) p 26.

39 Muhammad ar-Rifa'i personal reflection

40 Quran, 40:60

41 Thomas Moore, Dark Nights of the Soul. (Gotham Books, 2004) Introduction.

42 Quran 14:7

43 Muhammad ar-Rifa'i. Spiritual Medicine and Natural Remedies. (Sid Muhammad Press, 2003) p 16.

44 1 Thessalonians 5:16-17 (RSV)

45 https://drkirklaman.com/courses/heart-connection-meditation/

46 Quran 40:50

47 Imam Muslim. Sahih Muslim, Abdul Hamid Siddiqi, translator, 758 B.

48 Missing Reference

To experience The Remembrance, visit:
https://drkirklaman.com/courses-2/

You can download a free audio of
The Heart Connection Meditation and try
the technique yourself.

For more courses and blog posts, visit my main site:
www.drkirklaman.com

If you'd like further information about healing work through the heart, please contact the Institute of Spiritual Healing. They have a list of certified healers utilizing the techniques shared in *Inner Peace Now*.

https://instituteofspiritualhealing.com/certified-master-healers

www.ingramcontent.com/pod-product-compliance
Lightning Source LLC
Chambersburg PA
CBHW070141100426
42743CB00013B/2786